NATION-BUILDING

A Middle East Recovery Program

Jerry M. Rosenberg

University Press of America,® Inc.
Lanham · Boulder · New York · Toronto · Oxford

Copyright © 2003 by
Jerry M. Rosenberg

University Press of America,® Inc.
4501 Forbes Boulevard
Suite 200
Lanham, Maryland 20706
UPA Acquisitions Department (301) 459-3366

PO Box 317
Oxford
OX2 9RU, UK

ISBN 0-7618-2573-8 (clothbound : alk. ppr.)
ISBN 0-7618-2574-6 (paperback : alk. ppr.)

This book was completed just as the war against Iraq commenced. It does not, therefore deal with this confrontation, nor with its immediate causes. It is, however, related to the after-effects and follow-up, with issues of rebuilding, reconstruction, aid to the people of Iraq, the Middle East and the entire region.

J.M.R

"More than 50 years ago America won a war against European fascism, which it followed with a Marshall Plan and nation-building, both a handout and a hand-up - in a way that made Americans welcome across the world."

Thomas L. Friedman
The New York Times
March 19, 2003

"I like dreams of the future better than the history of the past."

Thomas Jefferson writing to John Adams, August 1, 1816

* * * * * * * * * * * * * * *

This Volume is Dedicated to

Ellen

my life-long partner and inspiration

and to

Lauren, Bob, Liz, Jon

the joys of daily living

and to

my extraordinary and loving grandchildren

Bess, Ella, Celia

"They are destined to witness a global spiraling; it will
fascinate them"

TABLE OF CONTENTS

PREFACE

PREFACE

In the spring of 1958, while studying in Paris, I heard Jean Monnet speak at the American Church, where he repeatedly praised the historic contributions of the famed World War II U.S. General, and later Secretary of State George C. Marshall. His central theme was that European recovery and reconstruction was made possible thanks to the generosity of the American people and to the 1948 Marshall Plan.

Monnet was the architect, who influenced French Foreign Minister Robert Schumann to support the establishment of a European Coal and Steel Community, initially between former enemies France and Germany. The 1958, Common Market (the Treaty of Rome) would lead the way towards an astounding European Economic Community. Today called the European Union it embraces the economies of 15 nations with its 375 million people consuming ¼ of all worldly manufactured goods. And it continues to enlarge, with 10 new nations expected to ascend in the year 2004.

It had been first my belief all along, now corrected, that economic integration of six nations of Western Europe was a grand strategy of rehabilitation following the destruction of the Second World War, and that Monnet and his handful of supporters alone promoted the concept of raising living standards by creating jobs and industrial growth as a means to keep the Soviet Union at bay as the Communists were moving westward in their conquest of Europe. I would learn that the United States was not only needed financially, but equally important, it was the conductor via the Marshall Plan, in this finely tuned orchestration of confidence building and nation-rebuilding.

*   *   *   *   *   *   *   *   *   *   *   *   *

Following the signing of the Oslo Agreement in 1993 between the governments of the Israelis and the Palestinians, a global commitment was made to move the peace process ahead, in particular with economic assistance as the glue to keep it on track. As an academic specialist in regional economic cooperation, I was asked to design models for economic integration in the Middle East, extending throughout the Arab-Muslim world of North Africa (Central Asia, though Muslim, was not considered as a relevant factor in the mid-1990s). Taking the forty-five year old success story of the European Economic Community and eliminating the warts while retaining the unique qualities of the present 15 nation-Union, I would apply this information to interact with other attempts at regional cross-border arrangements around the globe. It seemed rather straightforward, simple, so obvious, and so easy a transfer.

At the Middle East/North Africa Economic Summits held annually from Casablanca (1994), to Amman (1995), Cairo (1996) and the last in Doha (1997), I addressed small groups on a model for regional economic integration that would help sustain the region's peace.

Conversations were held with Israel's Prime Minister Sharon, and former Prime Ministers - Rabin, Peres, Netanyahu, and Barak; Palestinian Authority Chairman Arafat, King Hussein of Jordan, King Abdullah II-the present King of Jordan, Andre Azoulay-Senior Advisor to King Hassan and King Mohammad of Morocco, Turkey's Prime Minister Ecevit, President Karimov of Uzbekistan, and many others. They all convinced me of their sincerity in finding the correct path for regional economic cooperation.

Great personal moments came when Shimon Peres wrote in a private letter "To Jerry M. Rosenberg - With much respect for his attempt to organize a great dream". As early as 1995 Peres, reacting to my call for a Middle East Economic Community stated "I believe you have addressed yourself to the very foundations which will lie at the heart of the future of the region and I hope indeed that the day is not far off when the plan will be brought to realization."

Jordan's King Hussein personally acknowledged the legitimacy and possibilities of my initial model for an eventual economic community of Arab nations, working in harmony with Israel. The Executive Secretariat of the Middle East North Africa Economic Summit (based in Rabat, Morocco) asked me to write a book in time for the 1996 Cairo conference, describing my model of regional economic integration accompanying the flow of financial assistance.

What followed were meetings with dozens of prominent leaders from the Middle East, North Africa and the Central Asia region. Additional sessions were held with experts at The World Bank, The International Monetary Fund, the U.S. Department of State and at several U.S. Embassies.

Initially, the boundaries of this volume contained only nations of the Middle East and North Africa. With the attacks of September 11, 2001 and its aftermath, and an awareness of the interrelationships throughout the region following briefings at the U.S. Department of State, it seemed extremely appropriate to add the Muslim countries of Central Asia, Afghanistan, and Pakistan as potential partners.

President Bill Clinton in a personal letter earlier wrote "…as you point out, there is an opportunity to define the future of the Middle East in terms of reconciliation and coexistence rather than confrontation and violence. There are no limits to what can be done if the region's energy and talents can be channeled into creating new opportunities and building a land as bountiful and peaceful as it is holy." (August 7, 1996.)

*   *   *   *   *   *   *   *   *   *   *   *   *

This book, based on nearly a decade of pursuing the dream of a different, stable, and more prosperous Middle East, North Africa and Central Asia, with gradual, monitored, transparent cross-border economic integration rather than separation, presents in a timely and hopefully, objective fashion why a Middle East Recovery Program (MERP), not unlike the 1948 Marshall Plan, is now needed.

Natan Sharansky, Deputy Prime Minister of Israel during Prime Minister Sharon's first term in office, wrote to me on May 9, 2001 "As you know, I believe a recovery program for the countries of our region is of utmost importance. This program must bring not only economic growth, but also democracy, transparency in government and human rights to these countries, some of which are less than fully familiar with these concepts. I hope, by drawing on the 'Marshall Plan', you are able to formulate a blueprint that can succeed in the Middle East. I further hope that you are able to use the 'Marshall Plan' to illustrate to others how such plans have been successful in the past, and how, despite the daunting odds, such a plan could create economic growth, democracy, and peace in our region. I wish you much success in your important work."

Fully energized, I will now attempt to illustrate the pros and cons of MERP, as well as to transfer the Marshall Plan's remarkably, successful philosophy to a corner of the world, long lost to hate and poverty.

The Marshall Plan legislation of 1948 ran until 1952. Importantly, as one of its conditions, it gave birth to what we now call the European Union. The parallels are powerfully apparent. There could be a three-track approach in this rehabilitation/aid program - to commence initially with Palestinians in the West Bank and Gaza, then to include nations of the Middle East, then later to be added other Arab-Muslim and non-Arab Muslim nations. Or, although not my preference, it might start with Afghanistan, Central Asian nations, and spread westward.

Ideally, my studied preference would be to include, from the outset, all eligible Middle East, North Africa, and Central Asia countries, with participation a function of need and responsiveness to guidelines for the recovery program (it would be easy to later change the name from Middle East Recovery Program to Middle East/North Africa/Central Asia Recovery Program - MENACA).

This volume has been years in preparation, commenced long before the World Trade Towers and Pentagon attacks of September 11, 2001; before the September 2000 Aksa-Intifida crisis facing the peoples of Israel, the West Bank and Gaza Strip; before Saudi Arabia's Crown Prince Abdullah's call for a 22 nation-Arab League plan for a permanent peace with Israel; before President Bush's June 2002 pronouncements regarding Chairman Arafat and economic development for the Palestinians; before the campaign against Saadam Hussein, and before the release of the United Nations "Arab Human Development Report-2000."

Valuable information has been gleamed from recent news releases, and most critically from feedback following several invited briefings at the U.S. Department of State, The World Bank, and U.S. embassies where regional experts patiently sat with me during my attempts to explain the following models. Comments were fair, genuine, and most helpful.

In addition, travels to conferences and research centers in Morocco, Egypt, Israel, Jordan, Qatar, United Arab Emirates, Turkey, and Uzbekistan, have provided me with a critical insight and realization of the region's potential should peace and stability take hold.

Both Linda Biederman and Seth Hackman, promising MBA students at Rutgers University were most valuable by providing fresh ideas, a critical eye, and editorial suggestions.

I am also thankful to Ellen, my exciting, beautiful, loving, and accomplished wife of nearly 43 years, and to my children Lauren, Bob, Liz, and Jon, all of whom remain supportive of my interests and ongoing projects, and to my three young granddaughters-Bess, Ella, and Celia-who in their innocence, remain the playful hope for the future.

Lastly, the genius of those who, in 1947, wrote and argued for passage before the U.S. Congress of the European Recovery Program has largely been forgotten and unsung. In applying significant portions, with appropriate twists, I acknowledge their skills, tenacity, and dedication as they created a modern day masterpiece of historical proportion.

Tomorrow's events will assuredly produce rethinking of the following proposals and concepts. They are mine alone, to be defended by me, and when found in error, I alone am responsible and will apologize for the shortcomings.

Jerry M. Rosenberg   March 14, 2003
E-mail: rosenbrg@andromeda.rutgers.edu

CHAPTER I

INTRODUCTION

"The Middle East has always needed active American engagement for there to be progress, and we will provide it, just as we have for over half a century."

Colin Powell

Taskent, Bukhara, and Samarkand - the jewel of Central Asia's Islamic world, were unfamiliar places during a trip to Uzbekistan. The serene beauty of its mountains rivals the Himalayas, as do its deserts that are as dry as any on earth. Fertile valleys and visible oases dot the landscape of this beautiful region. Poverty, and especially drought, however, are arguably the most important causes of daily strife in this overwhelmingly Muslim nation of 26 million people.

Throughout Central Asia's history, water and trade have been dominant forces. The ancient "Silk Routes" linked China and Afghanistan with the West recalling fascinating stories of Alexander the Great passing through in the 4th C. B.C., as did

Genghis Khan in the 12th-13th century warlord who destroyed much of the early civilizations. Marco Polo arrived at the end of the 13th century and Tamerlane-the Uzbek national hero who by the 14th century had reached the western Afghan city of Heart.

Equally impressive, this area, inspired by Muhammad's trek from Mecca to Medina in 622 marked the start of an era of scientific discovery in the Islamic world producing a 500-year lead in science.

Commanded by the Koran to seek knowledge and read nature for signs of the Creator, and inspired by a treasure trove of ancient learning, Muslims evolved a society that in the Middle Ages was the scientific center of the world. The Arabic language was synonymous with learning and science for 5 centuries, a golden age that introduced the modern university, algebra, the names of the stars and even the notion of science as an empirical inquiry.

Muhammad's soldiers swept out from the Arabian Peninsula in the seventh and eighth centuries, annexing territories from Spain to Persia. They discovered the works of Plato, Aristotle, Democritus, Pythagoras, Archimedes, Hippocrates, and other Greek innovators.

And then, around 1600 it all came to an end; Western Europe took over and its Renaissance period was born. Islamic scholars that had won the world lead in science lost it at that time.

Four hundred years later, emerging out of the collapse of the Soviet Union in 1991, renewed attention focused on the 60 million people of the five countries in Central Asia. About ten years later, the terrorist attacks on September 11, 2001 and the subsequent bombing of Afghanistan have reinvented United States' involvement in the region. It will hopefully never wane again.

Thus with a broad sweep of the brush, the Middle East, as a geopolitical map has been permanently redefined. From Morocco on the westernmost end of the Mediterranean Sea, across North Africa, past Turkey and eastward into the heart of the Middle East, then swinging northeast to Central Asia, Pakistan and Afghanistan, half of the world's one billion Muslims, not all are Arab nations, few are secular and one is Persian, surround the land of 6 million Israelis.

The fifty-four year old, primarily Jewish state, known as Israel, remains embroiled by neighbors consumed by the challenge of a still-to-be born Palestinian country, a fresh reemergence of Intifada II uprisings, and failed negotiations.

History books will remind us how apparently simple it was back in the year 2000 when former President Clinton, meeting with Israel's Prime Minister Barak and PLO Chairman Arafat nearly concluded a peace agreement at Camp David. Today, that tiny corner of Israel's immediate neighborhood of 10 million, is now having its destiny geographically reconstituted by a wider expansion of countries into what we might call MENACA-the Middle East, North Africa, and Central Asia.

Following the Oslo Agreement of 1993, it became clear to many specialists that the Middle East conflict, or more specifically the feud between the Israelis and the Palestinians could be best resolved by widening the circle of engagement to include most Arab-Muslim nations. Thus, North Africa became a player in the peace process.

With the September 11th 2001 attack on the World Trade Towers and the U.S. Pentagon, the territory of consideration overnight expanded to include Central Asia, Pakistan and Afghanistan, seven countries with a primary, non-Arab-Muslim populace. Consequently, from that day forward, resolution and recovery of the Middle East would be impacted by events in North Africa, Central Asia, the Middle East, plus Afghanistan, Pakistan, and perhaps including Turkey. The fight against terrorism adds to the lexicon of variables.

Specialists in the region have been arguing ever since the disintegration of the Soviet Union that Central Asia was a part of the Middle East. Not only because of its geographic contiguity, through Iran, but also because of its constant shadow dance of diplomatic intrigues, commercial interests, religious fermentations and cultural frustrations, all of which are remarkably similar to those that define the Arab- Middle East.

David Fromkin, author of *A Peace to End All Peace* declared, "The Middle East, as I conceive it, means not only Egypt, Israel, Iran, Turkey, and the Arab states of Asia, but also Soviet Central Asia and Afghanistan..." (Fromkin, p. 16). Further complicating definitions, the U.S. Department of State continues, for historical reasons, to refer to the Middle East as the Near East.

Henceforth, there will be the "Middle East," with a capital "M" and a capital "E" to pinpoint contiguous neighbors of Israel. Then there will be the "middle east," with a lower "m" and "e", for those nations on the fringe that affect the outcome of the region's future.   It remains a huge territory of differing populations, cultures, languages, history, conflicts, expectations, and living standards.

Whether it be the United States, the United Nations, the European Union, Russia (the Quartet) or some combination, stabilization or nation-building in Afghanistan (and/or Iraq) will initially take precedent over other areas of the Middle East. That is to say, the creation of a Palestinian state and Israel's right of existence will go hand in hand with the Afghans long struggle following Osama bin Laden and more than 20 years of internal warfare.

Indeed, the United States must and will be forthcoming. In his insightful post September 11th 2001 article *Why Do They Hate Us?- The Politics of Rage*, Fareed Zakaria, *Newsweek* Magazine's International Editor argues that "To dismiss the terrorists as insane is to delude ourselves. Bin Laden and his fellow fanatics are products of failed societies that breed their anger. America needs a plan that will not only defeat terror but reform the Arab world." (Zakaria, p. 22).

In addition, hawkish theorists in the present Bush Administration support the democratic transformation of the greater Middle East. Deputy Defense Secretary Paul D. Wolfowitz sees a "liberated Iraq" as a vanguard of democracy, the first potential piece in a kind of reverse domino theory in which the United States could help foster the fall of authoritarian regimes in a reshaped Middle East..." (*New York Times, The,* 2003, Feb. 1).

* * * * * * * * * * * * * *

Have we learned our history lesson? Following World War II victorious leaders realized that the punitive Versailles peace treaty following World War I had helped pave the way for Hitler. (McCullough, p. 234). In 1948, the U.S. government established the generous, Marshall Plan (European Recovery Program) and it succeeded.

Now in the year 2003, President George W. Bush and other world decision-makers have called for strategies to begin reform and economic rebuilding in Afghanistan, in the Palestinian Authority, ultimately in Iraq, and perhaps throughout the region.

This volume examines the means of financial aid today and later gradual economic integration as a viable tool for reinventing a glorious past to make ascending nations, part and parcel of a great experiment to reconstruct a modern day crossroad of trade and peace. (Bar-El). A Middle East Recovery Program can be the glue that returns the entire region to a prosperity it has not seen for centuries.

One could argue for inclusion by, nation from the circumference, working carefully inward towards a nucleus, focused on the triangle of Israel, Jordan and Palestine. Counter claims are made to expand from a center outward towards an expansive complex of competing nations. Tradition has it that overlapping cultures shift ever so slowly away from a midpoint. Were this true, then Israel's position will defy this ruling as its background since its founding is grounded in Europe and not the Mideast.

Believing that a fitting long-term solution can only come about by resolving the Palestinian-Israeli conflict, this book first concentrates on that conflict, then reaches out across the geography of the landscape, to ultimately focus on models of treaties and free-trade agreements, to be signed in the march towards an expanded Middle East Economic Community, to include nations of the Middle East, North Africa, and Central Asia that fulfill requirements of ascendance.

THE MIDDLE EAST - ISRAEL AND THE PALESTINIAN AUTHORITY AND THEIR NEIGHBORS

The recently, accumulated evidence on Middle East, North African and Central Asian politics, as it deals with peace and cross-border regional trade and economics, supports the following beliefs:

. The United States, the European Union, other nations, and institutions, which are not part of the Middle East, such as the United Nations, have limited, but critical roles to play as facilitators, mediators, and/or as "honest brokers", and that any final outcome ensuring stability and security, must ultimately rest with the participants;

. The United States' greatest contribution today lies in being supportive of negotiations among all parties, and putting itself in the role as benefactor, as the primary contributor of financial assistance to help erase destitution, poverty, and unemployment for the impoverished citizens of those nations willing to halt aggressive ambitions against Israel.

. Timing is everything. The Oslo Accord generated excitement for nearly a decade sweeping people to search for a just and fair solution to the conflict. If the ideologies and plans of Oslo have run their course, or if Oslo is dead as some proclaim, then an alternative must be found.

. The Spring 2002 Saudi peace initiative, plus President Bush's June 2002 declaration on the Middle East conflict must interface with and respond to the strongly worded, competently prepared United Nations *Arab Human Development Report 2002* of July 2002. (UNDP).

The horrific violence in the region will someday end. Economic recovery assistance will be required, and should immediately be placed on the U.S. government's agenda for both dialogue and planning. Present day buzz words; "Regime-Change" and "Nation-Building" will ultimately be defined by action and then, reaction. The absence of one concept without thoughtful expectation of what is to follow is both reckless and unconscionable. The United States, the United Nations and all others in support of a future course of government must be responsible by forging specific programs that are both expensive and risky.

*　*　*　*　*　*　*　*　*　*　*　*　*

Jean Monnet, in the post-World War II era, spelled out a grand scheme of "containment" as a means to keep the nemesis of the past - the Nazis - within an organizational structure, by dealing with former and present "conflict", identifying national issues of "common problems" that would demand a "common management". Thus, his four C's. (Rosenberg, 1997, p. 134).

His great vision and ability to persuade was demonstrated in how French Foreign Minister Robert Schumann was able to take Monnet's vision for a peaceful and prosperous Europe to the French National Assembly, where he skillfully convinced a cynical group of politicians that an open, outreach effort with Germany, the former enemy of three major wars over 100 years, was the best route to an acceptable future for Europe.

Monnet's model of harmony via regional economic integration and his 4 Cs were envisioned by loosely defined state borders, by encouraging foreign direct investment and joint-projects, by witnessing via free trade accorded with their gradual lowering of tariffs and quotas that served as protectionist policies of pre-World War II days and as barriers to the promise of prosperity.

In addition to the commanding abilities and accomplishments of Monnet, and then Schumann to get the French Assembly and the citizens of France to agree to a dialogue and cooperative effort with the German government -

their former enemy of two world wars - was the United States government and its people providing monetary contributions.

The French writer, Raymond Aron, indicated that the prosperity of Western Europe would never have attained its present level of success were it not for the generous gift of the United States, envisioned in 1948 with Congress' European Recovery Program, most popularly known at the Marshall Plan.

"...But in point of fact direct investments in Europe by the American corporations did not go hand in hand with the Marshall Plan, but started to flourish only in 1955 and onward, that is to say several years later, attracted primarily by the acceleration of European growth and the prospect of the Common Market.... The objectives which the framers of the Marshall Plan set themselves were the rehabilitation of the ruined countries and the reconstruction of the European economies with a view to containing Communism and reducing the dangers of domestic subversion." (Aron, p. 190).

Critically, how can national economies best be integrated with former enemies? Can Israel accept an economic link with Iran, Iraq, Libya and others past and present, who continue to deny their right to exist? Was Israel's former Prime Minister Barak and his supporters correct with their pronounced strategy of survival by fulfilling the poetic justice of "Good fences make good neighbors," by justifying "separation" rather than "integration" with the desperate people of the West Bank and Gaza?

*   *   *   *   *   *   *   *   *   *   *   *   *

Further study and reflection reveal how wrong it was to believe that peace and prosperity on a long-term basis could exist without embracing former enemies.   The U.S. State Department Bulletin of May 8, 1949 contained Secretary of State Dean Acheson's claim: "The German stalemate heightened the general European crisis. The European Recovery Program could not succeed without the raw materials and finished products which only a revived German economy could contribute." (Pogue, p. 254).   Abandonment of past enemies, aside from the isolation that it creates, only exacerbates a messy situation. Conversely, a humbled nation currently on its knees is in time the best approach to wiping away past hatreds and misperceptions.

By the fall of 1947, the U.S. State Department realized that Europe needed immediate economic relief if there was to be any hope for later plans of recovery. President Truman appointed three special committees to study the impact on America of the proposed aid to Europe. The most important group, the President's Committee on Foreign Aid (chaired by Averall Harriman) enthusiastically endorsed what would be called the Marshall Plan. (Pogue, p. 217).

Then, on December 19, 1947, President Truman backed by bipartisan support and endorsements from special committees, asked Congress for the Marshall Plan: "The next few years can determine whether the free countries of Europe will be able to preserve their heritage of freedom. If Europe fails to recover, the peoples of these countries might be driven to the philosophy of despair - the philosophy which contends that their basic wants can be met only by the surrender of their basic rights to totalitarian control." (McCullough, p. 582).

The primary lesson was that the Marshall Plan paved the way for a genuine possibility to reinvent Europe with a future of stability and prosperity. Without the billions of US dollars in aid, Communism would possibly have taken control of the peoples and governments of Western Europe. Without the Marshall Plan, the one last hope for a new start in European life would have been impossible, assuredly a dramatic lesson heaped on today's Middle East.

As proven by the future condition of the Soviet satellite nations, Western Europe would have remained a disabled, sickly stepchild. Europe needed economic assistance, at least short-term, and we in the United States were willing and able to respond to her outreach.

Certainly, the forces, dynamics and times are very different in both the United States and in the Middle East, North

Africa and Central Asia. Some will question the need for aid to
the region; some will argue that the fear of communism no
longer presses forward.

Unfortunately, we are now faced with a more urgent
challenge, one that has finally come to our shores. There is
September 11, 2001 and a new reality facing the world as
threatened by terrorists from around the globe. They are our
newest enemies, with unrelenting anger, resentment and
determination. (In 1947, Marshall invited the defeated Nazi
Germany and the threatening Soviet Union to participate in the
European Recovery Program. Today the same debate will hold
true for our attackers - terrorists from around the world).

Furthermore, some will denounce the wastefulness of
funding to the generic area of the Middle East when the
corruption and misperception of western values only reacts with
terrorism; some will demand a protectionist viewpoint that this
regional hotbed is none of our business and butting-in will only
threaten our own stability and prosperity. History may repeat
itself with individuals leading the attack on the integrity of those
who search for a better life in the region, but they too will be
defeated.

Ideally, foreign aid and its organizational
implementation should follow cessation of all violence in the
area (this aside from military events that had been carried out in
Central Asia). New peace treaties with Israel's neighboring
states would assure rapid Washington acceptance. But,
realistically it cannot be expected that new peace overtures will
come soon.

The Marshall Plan of 1948 didn't make peace, for it
followed the conclusion of war. Still, the lexicon of peace is
more than just the end of killing. There is the peace of stability,
the peace from claiming victory over destitution and starvation,
the peace resulting from raising living standards, the peace
following recognition of another's right to exist, the peace of
trust, the peace of cooperation, the peace from transparency
along with government accountability, and critically, the peace

resulting from having basic institutions of governance and legitimacy in place, ready to absorb the flow of funds. Israelis and Palestinians may need to reach a sense of exhaustion, disgust, war-weariness, whatever, so that they would rather make compromises for differing definitions of peace than continue fighting.

There will someday be a state of Palestine. Equally true, no matter what attempts are made, by language or behavior, Israel will remain. Neither side is going to have a military victory, so the only way to end the conflict and killings is for both to agree to negotiate.

The alternative to waiting, witnessing, and merely studying events, is to commence preparation for a day that will arrive sooner, not later. Timed release of monies can be determined. Long-term aid should be tied to non-aggressive acts against, as well as peaceful overtures towards Israel (and vice versa). The promise of still more funding will assuredly stir participation.

The U.S. Department of State must maintain a vigil in the Middle East and never permit any void of commitment, including not being distracted by the ongoing fight against global terrorism. The Government of the United States, as a non-party to the conflict, especially remains the hope for peace and prosperity between the Israelis and the Palestinians, and consequently must maintain an announced willingness to rescue the region from violence and self-destruction with proper and fair funding.

The Economist magazine's (2001, p. 34) editorial noted that fifty years have passed since the soldier-statesman, General George Marshall, explained to Americans that urgent financial support for Europe would stabilize societies destroyed by the Second World War and would unleash Europe's potential for recovery to everyone's mutual benefit.

The Economist editorial called on the United States' new soldier-statesman Colin Powell to mobilize American technology and finances, both public and private, on behalf of the economic development of the world's poor countries that would be a fitting follow-up to the Marshall Plan.

Some nations will not qualify for funding at the outset; some will not wish to apply; some, with riches from natural resources will have too high a gross domestic product; some will be found with longstanding, uncontrollable corruption; some will refuse or be unable to cope with the stringent transparency requirements that will be set; and some, with continuing overt aggression towards Israel will not be eligible.

Islamic nations could benefit from MERP, but would they accept one from western hands? No matter the answer, it should not be said that any Muslim nation in the region, and Israel was at the outset not asked to share in this great experiment.

Funds from this recovery plan can go a long way towards restoring a more civil and just society throughout this wide Middle East region of more than ½ billion people. Those possessing both the wisdom and authorization will have to set priorities that some will find difficult to set, and which will assuredly be challenged. The list of expenditures of many billions of dollars, should go beyond the more traditional, appropriate, and obvious needs, such as humanitarian support, infrastructure development, housing construction, employment creation, educational building, etc.

The aid package presented in this book will demonstrate to the region and to the world that the United States remains committed to a universal hope for cultural and economic harmony among the 6 billion people of the world, of which as many as 1/2 billion are within the reach of MERP. The time to apply compassion, with an open wallet of assistance is upon us.

The pieces for resolution of Israeli-Arab conflicts are nearly in place. The Saudi peace initiative calls for normal relations of the 22-nation Arab League with Israel; President Bush envisions changes in the Middle East; and the UN's *Arab Development Report of 2000* pleads for global assistance. The Middle East needs the United States to lead the way, to show the worthiness of this investment for future peace. A Middle East Recovery Program could hold promise for a brighter future of stability and peace for the Israelis, Palestinians and other peoples living throughout the Middle East region.

CHAPTER II

BEFORE AND FOLLOWING SEPTEMBER 11, 2001

"We are the giant of the economic world whether we like it or not, the future pattern of economic relations depends upon us."

Harry S. Truman

Time, as it passes, can often be the ultimate healer. It can also be underutilized. If the United States is despised by some, not for what they do, but for what they represent by their successes, then comparative material failures in the once mighty civilizations of the MENACA region must be both frustrating and humiliating to its people. Assuredly, time can no longer be wasted.

BEGINNING WITH THE MIDDLE EAST, THEN....

In the pursuit of tomorrow, an eventual solution to the violence, terrorists, conflicts, killings, and perpetual threats in the Middle East must be within sight. The years of suspicion and mistrust focus on political strategies have been designed to wear out the other side, the announced protagonist. However, yielding to world pressures and the exhaustion of combat from both stones and bullets, encourages governments to seek reconciliation; to write a peace accord that will at a minimum avoid war-that is, the absence of killing; and to design a regional master plan dedicated to cooperation and prosperity.

Each generation of politicians mobilizes sufficient energy to seek a proper roadmap so as to provide for their citizens' security; each searches for that legacy of prominence and glory; each suspends programs from the most recent past in favor of newly minted, or reinvented venues.

Whoever resides in the seats of power, now Sharon-for a second term-in Israel and possibly Arafat in a future Palestinian state, eventually there will be an agreement to cease the fighting. This accord will replace years of anger and apprehension, upheaval and disruption, and a collage of suspended energies and failed opportunities that nearly closed the door of optimism and promise.

Help, including financial assistance for Middle East countries will be called for, perhaps sooner, definitely later, but assuredly it will be needed and requested. In the cry for assistance, will the United States, supported by other rich nations of the world, respond with favor and action? Leading to a generous and responsible response will demand a careful review of the requirements and the realistic expectations for rehabilitation and recovery. Likewise, the notes of history should remind all that the post-second World War destruction was not automatically reversed by Congress. It took great wisdom and courage, considerable stroking, and a handful of determined and assertive individuals to move the day's politicians to support the creation of the 1947 European Recovery Program.

Lessons from history remain for this day. An astute study of historical pendulums will hopefully reveal parallels in revisiting the post-1945 events of reconstruction. Understanding the pressure points of that period will give comfort, creativity, and practical ideas for evolving a program of uplift for another region of the globe - the Middle East and beyond- awaiting both vision and rescue.

Peace followed by donor assistance, could restore the Middle East to its role as a central actor in the world economy, enabling it to reclaim its unique geographic advantage between Europe and Asia. With demonstrated wisdom, decision-makers of the region can once again show that the Middle East has the potential to return to its past days of glory.

GLOBALIZATION BYPASSES THE MIDDLE EAST

Possessing excessive trade barriers, investment restrictions, regional fragmentation, commodity dependence, and trade policy isolation, the Arab people of the Middle East have watched the world leave them economically behind. (Bar-El).

A major United Nations report (UNDP) shows that progress in the Arab world has been made with life expectancy increasing by 15 years over the past three decades, and infant mortality has dropped by two-thirds. Arab income per head is higher than in most other developing regions and, combined, the 22 nations have less abject poverty (income of less than $1 a day) than any other developing region.

Nevertheless, there are significant problems:

(1) As the Arab world's (the 22 members of the Arab League) numbers continues to grow, rising from 175 million in 1980 to nearly 300 million people today, with the largest proportion of young people in the world (38 percent of Arabs are under 14) it is calculated that the population will top 400 million in 20 years.

(2) During the 20 year period, from 1980 to 2000 the Middle East's share of world exports declined from 13.3 percent to about 2.9 percent. Its share of world imports also dropped from 6.4 percent to 2.9 percent. (Gresser, p. 21).

(3) The region's share of world foreign investment has fallen by three-quarters since 1985, dropping from

4.8 percent to 1.6 percent.Arab total GDP, at $531 billion, is less than Spain's.

(4) One in five Arabs still live on less than $2 a day.

(5) Over the past 20 years, growth in income per head, at an annual increase of 0.5 percent, was lower than anywhere else in the world except sub-Saharan Africa.

(6) Around 12 million citizens, or 15 percent of the labor force, are unemployed; this number could rise to 25 million by the year 2010. (UNDP).

Country (or Region)	Population	Population % Growth	% Age under 15 Years	Life Expectancy in Years	Percent Muslim	Literacy Rate
Bahrain	645,361	1.73	30	73.2	100	85.2
Gaza Strip	1,178,119	4.01	50	71.01	98.7	--
Iran	66,128,965	.72	33	69.95	99	72.1
Iraq	23,331,985	2.84	42	66.95	97	58
Israel	5,938,093	1.58	27	78.71	14.6	95
Jordan	5,153,378	3	37	77.53	92	86.6
Kuwait	2,041,961	3.38	29	76.27	85	78.6
Lebanon	3,627,774	1.38	28	71.52	70	86.4
Oman	2,622,198	3.43	42	72.04	75+	80
Qatar	769,152	3.18	26	72.37	95	79
Saudi Arabia	22,757,092	3.27	43	68.09	100	62.8
Syria	16,728,808	2.54	40	68.77	90	70.8
UAE	2,407,460	1.59	29	74.29	96	79.2
West Bank	2,090,713	3.48	45	72.28	72.28	--
Yemen	18,078,035	3.38	47	60.05	--	38

* **Source - CIA - 2001 (July) World Fact Book**

Overcoming these significant problems ultimately rests with the leadership within Arab societies. Professor Fouad Ajami, a leading academic on the region boldly argues: "In the end, the battle for a secular, modernist order in the Arab world is an endeavor for the Arabs themselves." (Ajami, F. (2003) *Foreign Affairs*, p. 3).

EXPORTING TO THE SILICON VALLEY, NOT THE NILE VALLEY

United Nation's statistics reveal the critical role of trade relations where Palestinians were almost entirely dependent on trade with the Israelis. In 1998, according to the UN, over 96 percent of Palestinian Authority (PA) exports went to Israel. Then, in 1999, it dropped to 80 percent. A report issued by the United Nations since violence began on September 29, 2000 showed a devastated economy for the people of the Palestinian territories.

In December 2000, as reported by the International Jerusalem Post (2000), Terje Roed-Larsen, the United Nations Middle East envoy, in his report, pointed out that over a million Palestinians had suffered economic difficulty as a result of the uprising, "The harsh situation could lead to a regional war."

"Separation," as demanded by several past Israeli prime ministers, claims Saeb Erekat, the veteran Palestinian peace negotiator, "is a declaration of economic war." (*New York Times, The*, 2001, November 24).

Border closures have prevented Palestinians from working in Israel and the decline in gross national product reached $630 million for the year 2000, with income per capita down 11 percent. Palestinian Authority (PA) households were forced to reduce their savings, and the share of population living below the poverty line moved from 21 percent to 28.2 percent by the end of 2000. With the situation sustained through mid-2002, the poverty rate reached 43.7 percent, while unemployment in Gaza hit nearly 50 percent. (Seventy-eight percent of Palestinians in the Gaza Strip were unemployed by May 2002 according to a report said the number of unemployed reached 597,000 including more than 100,000 who worked in Israel before the current conflict, blaming Israel's closure policy for the high unemployment figures). Of the 1 million people in the Gaza strip, four-fifths fell below the poverty line, compared with one-third before Intifada II; more than half survived on emergency UN rations. As of August, 2001, two-thirds of the workforce were idle, compared with one-fifth before the Intifada, either because they could not go to jobs in Israel, or because local businesses had closed for lack of supplies and markets. With no solution yet found, and without swift financial assistance, an explosive situation carried out by desperate people and their sympathizers, could spill across neighboring borders, across the region, and eventually worldwide (*Jerusalem Report, The,* October 2001).

Trade between Israel and the Palestinian Authority fell by about $1 billion in 2002, compared to the previous year. Official commerce between the two sides amounted to $2.2 billion in 2001, and was $1.23 billion in 2002. Estimates of direct losses to the Palestinian economy since September 2000- including lost jobs in Israel and trade was roughly $4.5 billion. (*Jerusalem Report, The,* December 2, 2002, p. 108).

There is no way to comprehend the debate and emotions of the current Palestinian uprising without examining the moral, economic and social reality that the Israeli policy has created. With Oslo I and II, and expected self-rule under Palestinian Authority, the nearly 3 million Palestinians living in the territories hoped that the immense inequalities between themselves and the Israelis would be repaired or, at the minimum, that their lives would not be primarily controlled by an occupying government - Israel. Their unequal conditions did not end with Oslo, and in the ensuing years, further anger and hardship increased.

Even were Israel to lift the closures imposed on the Palestinian territories that prevent the free movement of goods and people, Palestinian economists believe that gains made in the Palestinian economy up to 2000 have already been wiped away. The concern of the experts is that any long-term investment projects will be replaced with short-term programs aimed at preventing poverty and coping with unemployment.

In 1999-2000, the Palestinian Authority had begun to recover from several years of a declining economy, but those gains are now gone. According to the World Bank, between January 1999 and June 2000, the Palestinian economy grew 6.1 percent compared with a 5.1 percent decline in 1995 and a 0.7 percent drop in 1998. The optimism continued in 1999 when 1,800 new companies were registered, with investment by the private sector valued at $350 million. (Bulmer).

Palestinians working in Israel helped bring unemployment down from over 20 percent to under 14 percent. But, with the Palestinian population of approximately 3 million in the territories (West Bank and Gaza Strip) and East Jerusalem growing at a world-high rate of 4 percent, job creation is an absolute necessity. (The United Nations foresees the population of the occupied territories rising from 3.3 million today to almost 12 million by 2050.)

More than half of the PA's international financial assistance has come from the European Union (the US has already given about one-quarter of the aid.) In October 2000, the European Union gave an emergency loan to pay the salaries of the PA's 100,000 or so employees. Then, in November, the EU transferred $23 million to the Palestinian Authority to provide Palestinians with money if Israel failed to honor commitments to transfer payments to the PA that was part of the Paris Economic Agreement signed by Israel and the Palestinians in 1994. "Israel is in breach of the Paris economic protocol," claimed Jean Breteche, the European Commission's representative in the West Bank and Gaza. (*New York Times, The*, November 2001).

At this time, citing security reasons, Israel suspended transfers of customs and value-added taxes that it collected on behalf of the Palestinians (some deputies claimed the money was helping to fund anti-semitic propaganda in the Palestinian schools.)

The EU stepped in and released 27.6 million euros (approximately $25 million) to help the Palestinians. Israel eventually resumed the transfers. The new EU loans were made available under its aid program for the southern and eastern Mediterranean.

Elsewhere, the United Nations Relief and Works Agency for Palestinian Refugees in the Near East (UNRWA-with its $ 736 million biennium budget and over 22,000 employees, provides assistance to 3.8 million registered Palestinian refugees in Jordan, Lebanon, Syria, the West Bank and Gaza) launched an "emergency appeal" to donor nations for $39 million to care for Palestinian refugees. Maher Nasser, as reported in The Economist (2001, January 6) the UNRWA liaison officer in Amman, said the money would help the agency provide emergency health services and treat the injured as well as provide relief operations including the distribution of food and other essential commodities. "UNRWA estimates that some 60,000 families in the West Bank alone are already in need of urgent food and cash assistance."

Palestinian refugees

PLACE	POPULATION	REFUGEES
Gaza	1,004,498	766,124
West Bank	1,596,554	652,855
Jordan	2,328,308	1,741,796
Lebanon	430,183	408,008

Syria	465,662	444,921
Saudi Arabia	274,762	274,762
Kuwait	37,696	34,370
Other Gulf	105,578	105,578
Iraq, Libya	74,284	74,284
Egypt	48,784	40,468
Other Arab States	5,544	5,544

Since 1948, close to $1.8 billion has been spent on the maintenance of Palestinian refugees throughout the region, with the United States contributing more than 60 percent of the UNRWA costs. (*International Jerusalem Report, The*). The Arab nations, had, until March 2001, provided little to the support of these people. (p. 42).

In February 2003, the United Nations Relief and Works Agency claimed that without immediate help it would run out of money to feed more than a million people, roughly a third of the Palestinian population, in the West Bank and Gaza Strip. Since the Intifada began in September 2000, there had been an increase of 115,000 people requiring assistance. (*New York Times, The*, 2003, February 11, p. A 10.)

In the first six years (1993-1999) of the Palestinian Authority (PA), when foreign aid donors provided more than $3 billion, Saudi Arabia and most other Arab states kept a conspicuous distance. Support from all of the Arab states combined rarely reached even 10 percent of total donations, and by design, almost none of it went directly to the PA, which was continually dogged by reports of corruption and mismanagement.

In November 2000, the Arab League agreed in principle to donate $1 billion (representing just 2 percent of the Arab countries' annual earnings from their investments abroad) to Palestinian aid projects. Nearly $700 million was quickly pledged to the fund. But by February 2001, only $10 million had been disbursed.

On March 19, 2001 the Persian Gulf oil nations announced a $300 million aid package to the PA, making Arab donors the Authority's chief source of budgetary support for the first time. Circulated via the Islamic Development Bank, up to $40 million a month for six months was to support a new "intifada fund" and head off bankruptcy of the PA. Most of the funding comes from Saudi Arabia, the United Arab Emirates and Kuwait. This amount was in addition to the previously unpublicized transfer of $80 million in Arab grants and loans to the Authority since December 2000. (Avineri).

The United States, on the other hand, barred by Congress from giving aid directly to the PA, contributed $57 million in January 2001 to Palestinian social programs.

During the frantic and horrific weeks of the fall-winter 2000-01, then Israel's Prime Minister Ehud Barak reaffirmed his position as he campaigned for reelection, on the February 6, 2001 election date. He wanted separation between the Israeli and the Palestinian economies, particularly in infrastructure, and believed that this could be achieved in three to five years, according to Yossi Kucik, Director-General of the Prime Minister's office. He was defeated in that election, replaced by Ariel Sharon.

(In August 2001, in his first diplomatic speech since his February defeat, former Prime Minister Barak asserted "If we do not separate from the Palestinians, this country cannot exist as a Jewish, Zionist and Democratic State." Apparently, even after being defeated Ehud Barak remained committed to separation.) *(Jerusalem Report, The; 2001, December 12)*.

Based on Israeli government estimates, the Palestinians' five-month offensive war cost them NIS (New Israeli Shekels) 3.4 billion (about $850 million). Costs included loss of income from Palestinian laborers who used to work in Israel (NIS 954 million); loss of trade with Israel (NIS 772 million); and the closure of the Jericho casino (NIS 247 million). (*Jerusalem Report, The,* 2001, December 12).

In fact, bilateral trade between Israel and the Palestinian Authority, which amounted to about $2.5 billion a year before the violence started in September 2000, had dropped off by as much as 50 percent. Israeli manufacturers and importers by year's end 2001 were selling little but food to the Palestinians. Sales of appliances and new cars dropped off to almost zero with the start of Intifada II. Almost all the trade that remains is in areas where the Palestinians have no alternative. Besides food, that includes buying fuel and electricity from Israel and depending on Israeli ports and airports to receive for most of the goods Palestinians purchase from abroad.

Then, in December 2001 Terje Roed-Larsen released another UNSCO report, (*International Jerusalem Report, The,* 2001) covering the first year of the uprising to the end of September, a period in which the West Bank was closed for two days out of three. In the last quarter covered by the report, severe internal closures were in force every day.

The closures meant that the Palestinian territories were in effect split into some 200 separate entities. Unemployment level had more than doubled from 11 to 25 percent, with an underlying jobless level of as high as 50 percent in the Gaza Strip.

The first year of the crisis, according to UNSCO had cost the Palestinian economy between $2.4 billion and $3.2 billion while Palestinian Authority revenues declined by 57 percent in the first nine months of the Intifada alone. With real incomes down by an average 37 percent, some 46 percent of the 3 million Palestinian population was living below the poverty line, double the pre-intifada figure.

*ISRAEL/WEST BANK AND GAZA

Israel		West Bank and Gaza
6 million	Population	3.2 million
125,000	Annual Births ·	129,000
19.12 percent	Birth Rate	35.48 percent
6 percent	Mortality Rate (under 5 years)	25 percent
264,000	Population (under 5 years)	595,000
79 years	Life Expectancy	72 years
96 percent	Literacy Rate for Females	69 percent
9 percent	Unemployment	40 percent
$110.2 billion	Gross Domestic Product	$3.1 billion
$1.1 billion	Foreign Economic Aid	$121 million
$31.5 billion	Import Revenue	$2.5 billion

*UNICEF, 2002; CIA World Fact Book

The UN analysis at the end of 2001 claimed that the economic situation was so severe that it was only donations from abroad, including from European Union and Arab countries, that were keeping the Palestinian Authority going.

Israeli incursions into the West Bank and Gaza Strip during March and April 2002 cost the Palestinians billions of dollars. Israeli soldiers had severely damaged the Palestinian economy and the infrastructure of the Palestinian Authority, according to the International Committee for the Red Cross, The World Bank and other international organizations. The World Bank, which is one of the largest donors to the Palestinian territories, estimated that the direct physical destruction of the public infrastructure $600 to $800 million. World Bank officials concluded that most of the developments from $5 billion of international donor aid to the Palestinians since the Oslo accords had been inappropriately used. The economic loss in gross domestic product alone was about $5 billion. (*Wall Street Journal, The,* 2002, April 29).

UN Special Coordinator for the Middle East Peace Process Terje Roed-Larsen noted that Israel's dismantling of the Palestinian Authority had left large swaths of the West Bank overrun by "lawlessness and anarchy." Ironically, at about this time, Prime Minister Sharon called for a Marshall Plan for the Palestinians. (Safire).

By the end of April 2002, UNRWA was distributing emergency rations to 90,000 Palestinians. Compounding the human disaster, the economy of the West Bank and Gaza was impoverished. The UN's economists estimated that three-quarters of all production in the West Bank had come to a halt, and that three-quarters of the workforce was either temporarily or permanently unemployed. The end of the Palestinian Authority was fast approaching.

"De-development" was the term used in the fall of 2000 by the United Nations Conference on Trade and Development secretariat to describe the "complex humanitarian emergencies," in the occupied territories. The continuing crisis had forced the PA into a heavy dependence on donor support for basic activities, "while diverting attention from long-term development goals and activities." (UNCTAD, October 7-18, 2002).

The United Nations Relief and Works Agency (UNRWA) in December 2002 issued an appeal to international donors for an additional $94 million for emergency relief work for the first six months of 2003. A third was earmarked for food aid to more than one million Palestinian people. Peter Hansen, UNRWA's commissioner-general, told donor representatives, "So rapid has been the humanitarian collapse that it will take an emergency program of the scale we present today to prevent a complete breakdown in Palestinian society." (*Financial Times, The,* December 12, 2002).

Christian Aid, a British charity, issued a report indicating that Palestinians were currently living in a state of extreme, worsening poverty and fear for their future. William Bell, the report's co-author said, "Almost three-quarters of Palestinians now live on less than $2 a day, below the United Nations poverty line." He said that doctors were reporting a sharp increase in child malnutrition, anemia in pregnant women, and underweight babies, as well as stress-related conditions, such as heart disease and hypertension. The organization also reported a 100 percent increase in new cases of mental health clinics since the start of the current Intifada, most of them children. (*Associated Press,* 2003, January 29).

Always sensitive to the casualties of conflict, Natan Sharansky, Deputy Prime Minister in Sharon's first government stated "By building democratic societies on the ruins of tyranny, the Marshall Plan helped create a prosperous and peaceful Western Europe. Now is a historic opportunity to do something similar for the Palestinians." Sharansky wants to help the Palestinian people by urging that the hundreds of millions of dollars in taxes being withheld from the Palestinian Authority during the Intifada be used as part of a kind of Marshall Plan to feed and care for the Palestinians so as to lessen their suffering. The monies would not go to Arafat, but rather through a humanitarian agency to the needy public. (*New York Times, The,* 2002, May 12).

CONSEQUENCES FOR ISRAEL

Economic fallout from disturbances in the region is likewise affecting Israel. There are plunging company valuations, rapidly disappearing cash reserves, and sorrowful venture capitalists. The share prices of most Israeli hi-tech firms have suffered considerably more than their U.S. counterparts.

For the first time in more than two years, the amount of venture capital into Israel dropped at the end of 2000. Company valuations for start-ups plunged by as much as 70 percent, meaning that founders and entrepreneurs have had to surrender more equity to outside investors to receive comparable amounts of cash they would have gotten in early 2000. (*Jerusalem Post, The*, 2000, December 20). In the last quarter of 2000, Israeli venture-capital funds increased their share of total hi-tech funding to 50 percent from 37 percent; a bad sign.

Likewise, closures have paralyzed dozens of Israeli construction projects and other joint efforts, as well as scaring away greatly needed foreign investment. The Israel Manufacturers Association said that Israeli companies marketing in the Palestinian Authority lost $250 million in the year 2000, based on a survey of damage to industry from the current violence. The study showed that 14 percent of the enterprises suffered severe damage, while 20 percent had moderate damage, since October 1st. (*Jerusalem Report, The*, 2001, October).

The contrast is both defining and sobering. In the first quarter of 2000, the Israeli economy grew by 5.1 percent; in the second quarter by 7.8 percent; and in the third quarter, prior to the outbreak of the new violence, the Israeli economy grew by an impressive 9.1 percent. Exports were up 48 percent; per capita gross domestic product reached $18, 643. For the year, Israel's GDP grew by 5.9 percent despite a fourth quarter drop to 8 percent, the sharpest single three-month decline in Israel's 52 year history.

For the year GDP per capita, at $17,700, set a record, up 3.4 percent from 1999; business GDP was up 7.7 percent, compared to a 2-percent rise in 1999. In 2000, Israel registered her lowest inflation rate in its history, the lowest rate in the world outside of Japan (which had negative inflation of 0.7 percent.)

In addition, the year 2000 set a record for foreign investment in Israel. Total direct and financial foreign investment had been $8.6 billion since the start of the year, 1.5 times the $5.58 billion raised in 1999. However, there was a sharp ebbing of foreign investment beginning with October during the disturbances in the territories. The total investment of foreign citizens in Israeli securities and real estate, for example, fell in November to an all-time low of $128 million. The outbreak of violence had sent foreign investment down from $417 million to only $250 million. In August, the total was $1.2 billion, while the year's high was recorded in March at $2.3 billion. (*Ha-aretz*, 2001).

In a further indication of the declining situation in Israel, a special Business Data Israel (BDI) study of trends in investment in the Israeli market by foreign companies and concerns shows that the sum of these investments declined from $60.2 billion on December 31, 2001 to $53.8 billion on December 31, 2002, a 10.6 percent decrease. (*Globes*, 2003, January 26).

The Federation of Israeli Chambers of Commerce reported that "The Israeli economy is hardly dependent on trade relations with the Palestinian economy. Total exports to the Palestinian territories account for only 8 percent of total exports. Even today, most export-led activity to this region continues to be conducted, since the Palestinians are absolutely dependent on Israel for its supply of basic food products and other commodities.....In the first nine months of the year (2000), private foreign investment activity in Israel has doubled, while foreign investments in Israeli securities have grown four-fold compared to the same period last year. Even after the recent security-related events, no clear downtrend in the business activity between Israel and abroad has been noted, or the pulling out of investors from Israel for that matter." (*Jersualem Report, The*, 2001, December 12).

However, the Federation, in its reverse to this optimism claimed that the current unrest, had already cost Israel over $1 billion, amounting to a loss of 1 percent of Israeli GDP. The Israeli Tour Guide Association reported that some 2,000 of its 2,500 registered tour guides were without work. According to the Federation, "Today, the Israel economy enjoys unprecedented economic strength and increasing stability in its macro-economic frameworks. This is reflected in the main economic indicators, namely a steady slowdown in inflation, price stability comparable to European markets, a marked reduction in the budget deficit and a reduction in the weights of the total debt and public spending as percentages of the GDP."

Tourism continued to drop in January 2001, by 16 percent. The average hotel occupancy rate was less than 40 percent, with the greatest drop in Jerusalem and in the North of Israel, followed by Tel-Aviv (on the other hand, hotels in the Dead Sea were packed, not necessarily with tourists, but instead mostly with Israelis whose stay were subsidized, thus keeping staff employed, and guests happy.) In September 2000, 350 hotels were operating in Israel, totaling 46,500 rooms. One year later, thirty hotels, with 2,500 rooms had closed. (*Jerusalem Report, The*, 2001, December 12). The number of foreign tourist bed nights was the lowest since 1967, with hotel occupancy for the year 2002 at 40 percent, the poorest yearly average ever recorded. (*International Jerusalem Post, The*, 2003, February 7, p. 21).

A total of 862,300 visitors from abroad entered Israel during 2002, making it the worst year for tourism in 20 years. The figures for 2002 were 29 percent lower than those for 2001 and two-thirds lower than those recorded in 2000.(*International Jerusalem Post, The*, 2003, February 7, p. 7).

Foreign shipping companies that used to make occasional calls at Israeli ports were refraining from doing so due to fear of the Arab boycott and/or out of concern that insurance firms would charge a war levy due to the security situation making it economically unfeasible to stop in Israel. These shipping companies do not have permanent offices in Israel, but their ships used to call at Israeli ports every few months to deliver various consignments while visiting regional ports. Recent attempts to ship consignments through these companies were turned down, and it was understood that the refusal stemmed from newest apprehension over the Arab boycott. (Sher).

Exports to Arab countries plunged 39 percent in the spring 2002. Exports had reached $21.3 million with the largest drop of 47 percent ($12.1 million) to Jordan, Israel's largest trading partner in the Arab world. (*International Jerusalem Post, The*, 2002, May 31).

The ongoing Intifada and the post-September 11th terrorist attacks would cause at least $7.5 billion in overall damage to the Israeli economy in 2001-2002. (*Ha-aretz*, 2002). The fallout from the World Trade Towers and Pentagon attacks were expected to have a relatively small impact on the Israeli economy, compared with the U.S. and other Western countries, totaling $562 million, or 0.5 percent of GDP. A loss 0.2 percent of GDP was expected due to the drop in demand for Israeli exports, while each 10 percent decline in Nasdaq stocks represented a loss of 0.1 percent of Israeli GDP. Further damage, assessed at 0.1 percent of GDP, was to be caused by the fall in private consumption. The additional damaged expected in 2002 was to come on top of a loss representing 4-4.5 percent of GDP due to the Intifada and the deep high-tech crisis. The overall damage caused by the Intifada (*Jerusalem Post, The*, 2002, April) was to be 2 percent of GDP, while the high-tech crisis impact was estimated at 2-2.5 percent of GDP.

In November 2002, it was announced in a government report that one in five Israelis was living in poverty. (*Economist, The*, November 9, 2002, pp. 49-50.)

*   *   *   *   *   *   *   *   *   *   *   *   *

The year 2002 closed out with bad news. The Central Bureau of Statistics reported that gross domestic product contracted for the second straight year. After record growth of 7.4 percent in 2000, GDP shrank by 0.9 percent in 2001, and an additional 1 percent in 2002, making it the worst on record since 1953. Other critical indicators, such as consumer spending and per capita GDP, also declined, while unemployment hit a depressing 10.4 percent, with 265,000 people out of work. That was a rise of 1 percentage point since the end of 2001. (*International Jerusalem Post, The,* 2003, January 10, p. 7).

In addition, inflation increased to 6.5 percent for the entire year 2002, the highest since 1998. The rise in inflation was more than double the government's 2 percent-3 percent target following two years of very low inflation, 1.4 percent in 2001 and zero in 2000). (*International Jerusalem Post, The,* 2003, January 31, p. 20).

(Further exacerbating the situation, the Israeli economy could lose $1 billion, if and when war breaks out in Iraq. The estimate assumes a 1 percent loss of GDP, similar to the loss in the 1991 Gulf War, which cost the Israeli economy $650 million) (*Globes,* January 20, 2003).

ISRAEL'S CLOSEST NEIGHBORS

Across the river in Jordan, workers were also suffering. Jordanian businessmen had bet on the peace process, spending over $1 billion on building hotels after 1998. A 40 percent drop in western tourists means that most of the hotels were either half-finished or half-empty.

Jordan expects the country's economic growth to barely match its population growth of 3.3 percent.

According to Omar Salah, a leading Jordanian entrepreneur, before the latest wave of violence, about half of all Jordanian businessmen carried on some type of cross-border trade with Israeli firms. That percentage had plummeted to only 5 percent.

Nevertheless, 36 year old Omar Salah remains optimistic "Listen there has obviously been a breakdown between the two sides, but there is going to be a cessation of violence sooner or later...Compare the situation to the Marshall Plan in the aftermath of the Second World War. Instead of ostracizing Germany, the allies helped rebuild the economy of Germany and helped bring Germany back into the economy of Europe. In the long run, this approach was much more successful than the reaction of the victors following World War I....Similarly here- once the second intifada dies down, we will have to try something different from what was done following the first one." (*Pharaohs*).

Opportunities for Jordan remain high. Her exports to 115 non-Arab countries rose by 19.7 percent to $1.1 billion in 2001, selling $884.2 million the previous year. There was a significant jump in U.S.-bound exports from four Jordanian-Israeli industrial zones. (Gresser, p. 6).

Egypt, along with Jordan, has a peace treaty with Israel. Nevertheless, based on 2001 figures, unemployment remains at 9 percent. Egypt requires half million new jobs each year as the population increases by 3,655 per day. She also has more natural gas (about 1 percent of the world total) than she can use and wants to earn badly-needed hard currency by exporting gas. The natural market right next door, is Israel, but Israel was put off limits until the Israelis and the Palestinians remain in conflict.

One ideal way to build Egypt's economy would be to build a natural gas pipeline that connects Egypt to Israel, a huge gas consumer, and then build north and east to other countries. With strong Palestinian sentiment among Egyptians, the participation of Israel is doubtful; this severely impacts Egypt's plans to spend needed funds for pipelines that bypass Israel, the largest gas consumer in the region.

The developers who initially conceived of building Egypt's first private airport had visions of tourists by the thousands coming to a new $1.2 billion resort on Egypt's southern Red Sea coast. But when the Marsa Alam International Airport opened in early November 2001, it attracted just one weekly fight, from Germany.

Tourism, the government's largest source of revenue, is crucial to Egypt's economy. In 2000, the country drew 5.4 million visitors worth $4.3 billion, accounting for 10 percent of Egypt's gross domestic product. About 2.2 million of Egypt's citizens have jobs related to tourism.

· As soon as the violence began between Israelis and Palestinians, Egyptian tourism started slipping. In the first half of 2000, (before Intifada began in September 2000), 430,000 people came from Israel, but fewer than 37,000 came in the first half of 2001. In addition, one month after the September 11th attacks on the U.S., tourist activity dropped nearly 45 percent. (*Pharaohs*).

From the Jordan River to the Mediterranean Sea live 4 million Palestinians - one million Israeli citizens; 200,000 Palestinians who reside in East Jerusalem and another 2.8 million who live in the West Bank and Gaza Strip. In reality, the combined 10 million Israelis and Palestinians inhabit a single geographic state controlled by one government, living under two separate and unequal systems of rights and regulations.

CENTRAL ASIA AND ITS NEIGHBORHOOD

Before the U.N coalition October 2001 bombing, Afghanistan was one of the poorest nations in the world. Few schools or hospitals existed, one in four children died before reaching the age of 5, three-quarters of her 26 million citizens could not read and the country lacked health facilities, such as safe drinking water and sewerage systems, and average life expectancy was 40 years. When it comes to basic physical needs for survival, Afghanistan lacks them. (United Nations' estimates for rebuilding Afghanistan include a cost up to $6.5 billion for thirty months following the October bombing.) (*New York Times, The*, 2003, January 31).

The nations of Central Asia are in a similar situation. With a combined population of 60 million people and an average GDP per capita of U.S. $3,100 poverty is rampant. (CIA, 2001).

Some data regarding Central Asia, Pakistan, Turkey, and Afghanistan * -

Country (or Region)	Population	Pop-ulation % Growth	% Age Under 15 Years	Life Expect-ancy in Years	% Muslim	Literacy Rate
Afghanistan	26,813,057	3.48	42	46.24	99	31.5
Kazakhstan	16,731,303	.03	27	63.29	47	98
Kyrgyztstan	4,753,003	1.44	35	63.46	75	97
Pakistan	144,616,639	2.11	40	61.45	97	42.7
Tajikstan	6,578,681	2.12	41	64.18	85	98
Turkey	66,493,970	1.24	28	71.24	99.8	85
Turkmenistan	4,603,244	1.85	38	61	89	98
Uzbekistan	25,155,064	1.6	36	63.81	88	99

* Source - CIA - 2001 (July) World Fact Book

Without the building blocks for a "new society," not only will aid probably fail to produce positive results, indeed, it may backfire and increase discontent and for most of the people, increase poverty. Specialists will be needed to educate the masses on issues of freedom, capitalism, banking, schooling, cultural opportunities, etc. Acceptance by the people of the US's outreached hand is not automatic.

During the October 2001 bombing campaign, President Bush arguing that following the military victory the US could not just walk away, approved an initial $320 million in aid for

Afghanistan, with more to come. These monies would be used to feed the more than three million refugees who had left the country prior to the coalition bombing and another 1.5 million starving people crossing the borders into Pakistan and Iran. (*New York Times, The,* 2001, November).

PAKISTAN

Once disbursed, funds would be used for infrastructure needs-roads, bridges, electric plants, water treatment facilities; then schools and hospitals. Ultimately, the recovery program would help finance institutions, governance, a legal system, the formation of political entities, election procedures, a banking system, federal means for tax and customs collecting, internal and external trade, and the list continues.

Pakistan is awash in drugs, guns, refugees and mounting anarchy is both poor and anxious to receive attention and funding from the United States following their cooperation in the coalition against the Talibans. The lack of stability during and following the coalition bombing in Afghanistan frightened Pakistan's foreign customers, raised freight-insurance charges and contributed to an uncertainty that hurt her economy. Short-term losses in trade, manufacturing, foreign investment and government revenue amounted to nearly $2 billion by the end of 2001, with economic growth for the fiscal year down a full point to 2.5-3.1 percent.

Pakistan, with $38 billion of foreign debt, (*Wall Street Journal, The,* 2001, November 12) even with new loans and easier terms on old ones suffered significantly during the months leading up to and following the September 11th attack on the U.S.:

Period	Exports '000 tons	Imports '000 tons
September 1- 10, 2001	18.9	$ 71.1
September 11-30	19.5	59.4
October 1-15	12.4	59.9
October 16-31	12.9	58.0
November 1-7	9.9	49.1

CENTRAL ASIA

Arguably, the newest post September 11, 2001 strategic partners became the former Soviet republics of Central Asia. Financial assistance would also be needed to overcome their poverty, corruption and lack of infrastructure. For example, Tajikistan, the region's poorest country is a central corridor for heroin smuggling; Uzbekistan has one of the worst records of human rights in the region; Kazakstan, has emerged as one of the world's biggest new sources of oil, attracting billions of dollars of investment from drilling and pipeline companies.

Indeed, the World Bank, has loaned $3.5 billion to Central Asian nations in the 10 year period (1990-2000) with an additional $1.5 expected in the following decade. The European Bank for Reconstruction and Development likewise plans to invest $300 million over several years to these nations following 2001. The United States, on its own, plans to provide hundreds of millions of dollars in new assistance after 2001. (*New York Times, The*, 2001, November).

NORTH AFRICA

The African nations on the southern rim of the Mediterranean Sea include Morocco, Algeria, Tunisia, Libya, and Egypt. The Sudan is at times included. Egypt has a dual geographic identity, also being a nation of the Middle East.

North Africa data* -

Country or Region	Population	Pop. % Grow th	% Age under 15 Years	Life Expectancy in Years	% Muslim	Literacy Rate
Algeria	31,736,053	1.71	34	69.95	99	61.6
Egypt	69,536,644	1.69	35	63.69	94	51.4
Libya	5,240,599	2.42	35	75.65	97	76.2
Morocco	30,646,305	1.71	34	69.43	98.7	43.7
Sudan	36,080,373	2.79	45	56.94	70	46.1
Tunisia	9,705,102	1.15	29	73.92	98	66.7

* Source - CIA - 2001 (July) World Fact Book

North African nations long subdued by their former colonists, France and England, are today determined to reach out and find new export opportunities throughout the world. In particular, Morocco, Algeria, Tunisia, Libya, and Egypt are finding a greater reception not only in Europe but also in the United States, countries throughout Asia, other nations of the African continent, and South America.

Surprisingly, a loss of trade with their former colonists has, more than adequately, proven successful. Their exports have increased along with profits.

Special attention in recent years has been given by these countries towards fulfilling ISO-9000 manufacturing requirements, thus providing increased acceptance.

ISRAEL'S FAILED APPROACH

Former Prime Minister Ehud Barak often quoted America's distinguished poet Robert Frost "Good fences make good neighbors" as he called for a trial separation that he said might also become permanent. His key staff busily prepared contingency proposals in which Israel would separate unilaterally from the West Bank and Gaza should a peace accord not be realized. As conceived, the draft of the plan called for Israel to withdraw its soldiers from some areas of the West Bank, stake out new borders, and ultimately erect barriers along these boundaries, with carefully controlled crossing points. To the former Prime Minister Barak, political and geographic border separation would have promoted a "healthier relationship" between the two peoples. (*Ha-aretz*, 2001).

"If it becomes clear that there is no partner for peace on the other side, we will go for unilateral separation," Barak informed a parliamentary committee. His planners had already recommended a permanent militarized border between the two entities, a strategy for replacing Palestinian workers with mostly unemployed or underemployed Israelis, and for disentangling villages. So there is no way to execute a separation, except by establishing two parallel grids, which could never be done.)

With Ariel Sharon as Israel's Prime Minister following his February 6, 2001 election victory, (he would be re-elected in January 2003), revised definitions and approaches to separation and closures, were his to make. By the summer 2002, Sharon had created buffer zones and was installing cement and electronic walls along the Green Line with the West Bank. (*Ha-aretz*).

*   *   *   *   *   *   *   *   *   *   *   *   *

PA Chairman Arafat, as he awaited the new Prime Minister Sharon's strategy in early March 2001, had already rejected Barak's plan for economic separation, saying he supported only a "political separation that is based on the 1967 border, international resolutions and...will lead to the setting up of a Palestinian state." (The last time Palestinians rejected separation was November 29, 1947, when the United Nations announced the partition of Palestine, leading, the following May, to the establishment of the State of Israel.) (McCullough, p. 611).

Ever since 1967, when Israel took control of the West Bank and Gaza with its then 2 ½ million people, Israel has been the arbiter of Palestinian economic development. Following the Oslo peace accord in 1993, Israel continued to retain ultimate control of every exit and entry point for goods and people in and out of the Palestinian territory. The result, while Israel's economy flourished with a per capita income of $17,700, the Palestinians earned less than $2,000 a year. In the past decade alone (1991-2000), the disparity increased, with the average Israeli income more than doubling and the Palestinian earnings remaining flat. (Sher).

Today, in 2003 and a re-elected Ariel Sharon, the borders between Israel and the West Bank and Gaza are reminders of the years of division between the West- and East Germans, separated by barbed-wired walls and army sentries on alert duty. The Palestinian landscape contains ruins of incomplete joint-projects that were built on the dreams of peace integration.

The blue-prints of vast cross-border schemes, many first presented following the Oslo agreement, at the four annual Middle East/North Africa Economic Summits held respectively in Casablanca, Amman, Cairo and Doha, are curtailed, halted, or cancelled. Glossy booklets and architectural blueprints were prepared for these forward-looking global conferences, and now are collecting dust on bookshelves. (Rosenberg, 1996).

THE EUROPEAN UNION'S ROLE

During the positive years following Oslo, the European Union had committed monies to their neighbors across the Sea. On November 28, 1995, in Barcelona, Spain, the EU and its 12 southern Mediterranean partners created a new policy framework - the Euro-Mediterranean Partnership. (Rosenberg, 1997, p. 126) The European Union promised $4.1 billion over five years to help nations on the southern rim. This was equal to 70 percent of the aid offered to Central Europe's countries. By the end of 1999, only 26 percent of that commitment had been paid out. Yet to the remaining 74 percent, the EU decided to add another $4 plus billion for a program lasting through 2006.

The EU's initiatives in the Arab world are based on the Euro-Med or Barcelona process, which, since 1995, was to bring southern rim nations of the Mediterranean into free trade relations. In addition, the EU has continued to work to bring the Gulf Cooperation Council nations into closer trade relationships.

The cornerstone of the Euro-Mediterranean partnership is the establishment of a large free trade zone around the Mediterranean basin by the year 2010 to ensure the prosperity of the region. In essence, this entails dismantling the tariffs that the Mediterranean countries impose on imports from the European Union, since they already enjoy comprehensive duty-free access to the EU for their manufactured goods.

Nearly $6 billion (far greater than US funding) were invested by 15 nations of the EU in the 12 Mediterranean countries in 1998. Almost one third went to Israel, and another

25-30 percent to oil and gas exploration and distribution in countries such as Algeria, Egypt, Tunisia, and Syria.

Intra-regional trade remains still significantly low, and high customs barriers protect small markets. Thus the entire Maghreb market (Morocco, Algeria, Tunisia, Libya and Mauritania) corresponds only to the size of the internal Portuguese market. (Rosenberg, p. 210). Assuredly, there is a need to spur sub-regional integration in the Mediterranean as a whole, and in the Maghreb in particular, is paramount.

ISRAEL'S STRATEGY UNDER BARAK

At the outset of the year 2000, the government of Israel prepared a plan for a regional cooperation association of nations to shape a new framework for relationships between countries. (Robson). Modeled after the Association of Southeast Asian Nations (ASEAN), the plan called for international disputes to be solved through talks and without incitement, as well as the pursuit of regional economic cooperation and security. By January 2001, everything was put on hold.

Israel's major free trade agreements include the European Union Free Trade Agreement (EU FTA); the United States of American Free Trade Agreement (USA FTA); the European Free Trade Association Free Trade Agreement (EFTA FTA): and many more. These accords provide unparalleled access to the world's most important markets, in particular, Israel has tariff-free entry to both the U.S. and the European Union.

As late as September 2000, Israel and the Palestinian Authority appeared close to establishing a Free Trade Area (FTA) as part of their final economic accord. "But first," spoke Oded Eran, Barak's one-time peace negotiator, an "effective economic border" needs to be established. Eran explained that an interim period would be required to enable the two sides to prepare the administrative infrastructure and work out the details for the new economic border arrangement. The final agreement was to provide for the free, although monitored movement of workers between the Palestinian and Israeli economies. Assuredly, this

FTA was based on economic separation, with each side enjoying economic independence. By January 2001, everything was put on hold. (*Ha-aretz*, 2001).

The brake was pulled by Mohammed Isktayyeh, the Palestinian official negotiating on economic affairs who noted that it was premature to say that there had been an agreement in principle since "everyone knows the economic scenario comes after the political." (Sher).

Gamemanship had won. Beginning with November 2000, the optimism of creating a free trade agreement, of integrating the economies of the region, and of pursuing the impressive goals of Oslo had all but reversed The talk was that Oslo was assuredly bleeding and near death.

STRATEGIES UNDER SHARON AND POWELL

Assuredly, Ariel Sharon, elected prime minister of Israel on February 6, 2001 (taking office one month later following the formation of a unity government) set his own agenda, which included a close examination of policies of former governments. The crisis in the region, and the downfall of Ehud Barak, after only 21 months in office, clearly revealed to a great upheaval period.

Sharon was aware that the Palestinians, as well as the Israelis, are here to stay, neighbors to the end, whether friendly or antagonistic. Any complete unilateral separation would be problematic for a host of reasons. To begin with, by design, Israel made the Palestinians dependent on them, as seen by the grid patterns for electricity, telephone connections, etc. Condemnation would be heard around the world were Israel to deny the Palestinians their critical sources of supply.

If separation were the ultimate solution, then the question must be what form of separation would be best. Is "separation with cooperation" the likely outcome? This form of independence between Israelis and Palestinians, is in all probability to follow an agreement, including Israel guaranteed its security and the state of Palestine guaranteed its own separate economy. The result will, by necessity, require the creation of a free trade zone - free of customs, tariffs, quotas and other trade barriers. Both Israel and the Palestinians would be free to determine their own tariffs and to sign trade accords with the Arab World.

A free-trade agreement between the governments of the Israelis and the Palestinians would in all probability require the inspection of goods at the crossings. Inevitably, the border stations would cause delays and increase the costs of trade, but the tradeoff would be security and allowing both sides control over the quality of goods entering them.

And what of Gaza and the West Bank, separated by the land mass of Israel proper? A route must be constructed to enable Palestinians to move and to trade freely between the two regions and bypass any interaction with Israelis. In all probability, the solution will be found with a super-highway bridge someday connecting the divisions of the nascent state of Palestine.

In addition, there is a need to promote bi-national industrial parks in order to encourage and enable cooperation between Israelis and Palestinians. There is also a need to create foreign enterprises that include work for Palestinians within designated zones. A typical park would have entrances on each side of the border, where certified laborers would freely enter. With this approach, any closure for security reasons would be unnecessary.

Over time this may lead to a gradual reduction in the number of Palestinians working in Israel. In turn, this would prevent a situation where many Palestinians are vulnerable and could lose their jobs on the spur of the moment. By design, it would require the PA to anticipate a solution to the problem created by designing jobs in the West Bank and Gaza with its own industry. To fulfill this goal, foreign investment would be required, that could serve as another incentive to maintain the peace. The end objective would be Palestinians and Israelis accepting the reality that they must learn to live together. This security and stability would be based on a strategy of cooperation through separation. (Sher).

Is it possible to cut the links between the Israeli and Palestinian economies, forged over three decades? Yes, but the links were designed to be ties that bound the two peoples together. After thirty-three years of occupation, their economies are presently, closely interlinked and are creating benefits daily to both sides. Some links could be readily severed, but attempts to severe them would only create larger problems for both sides.

Colin Powell, on his first Middle East trip as U.S. Secretary of State in mid-February 2001 raised the possibility of an administrative collapse in the Palestinian Authority. Powell said this could contribute to the escalation of the conflict with Israel. He also added that economic pressure by Israel did "nothing to improve the security situation." (*Ha-aretz*, 2001, February). The trade blockade on Palestinian areas remained a blunt instrument that did more to incite Palestinian outrage and the concomitant escalation of violence. If indeed as many claimed that the Oslo process was dead, then Powell's statements suggesting that he was willing to look at the Israeli-Palestinian conflict through fresh eyes, was promising.

Sharon's response was that he would allow Palestinian employment in Israel, but only following the cessation of violence. Complicating matters, there was a grave concern, though unproven, that Chairman Arafat was interested in further deterioration so that the possible breakup of Palestinian rule would result in international intervention. No matter what the mistrust, sustaining a certain standard of living for the Palestinians was and remains a clear-cut national and security priority in the PA.

Based on the economic situation by early Spring 2002, it was quite conceivable that a Palestinian welfare state was likely. Additional aid of $1 billion, or more, from the United States, the European Union, and other humanitarian-offering nations would be needed to keep the West Bank and Gaza afloat and functioning. More monies would assuredly be required.

Much changed with the increased suicide-bombings in Israel by the summer of 2002. Prime Minister Sharon had surrounded Chairman Arafat's compound and was well into a program of adding buffer zones and constructing cement and electric walls around much of the West Bank.

(At a meeting in Jerusalem late in February 2002, Prime Minister-elect Sharon and other senior government, military, and corporate officials, discussed that the severe economic plight in the territories had already caused the complete paralysis of many of the Palestinian Authority's institutions. Without the money, goods, and raw materials that flow from Israel into the West Bank and Gaza Strip, the condition was likely to degenerate into mass starvation, collapse of organizational units, and a concomitant escalation of violence.)

Shimon Peres, foreign minister in Sharon's first government had no illusions, but he did have plans - a partial reinvention of his existing vision for a new Middle East. According to *The Jerusalem Report* (2001, October) he would begin pushing to:

a. make significant changes in the economic condition of the Palestinians, since the present crisis was encouraging PA citizens to join the terrorists. Peres believed that, without economic revival in the West Bank and Gaza Strip, the conflict would continue and expand;

b. re-open selective closures permitting Palestinian workers back into Israel;

c. transfer funds owed by Israel to the PA;

d. increase international contributions to the PA; and

e. create a long-term joint common market for Israel, the Palestinians, and Jordan.

Unlike the Prime Minister, Peres was willing to suggest these strategies, before the violence had subsided, an approach that was believed would also comfort governments around the world.

APPROACHING CHAOS

$2.4 million each day, had been lost because resulting from the closures along the borders between Israel and PA. Palestinian unemployment, which even in ordinary times was high, had tripled to 38 percent since the beginning of the so-called Alaksa Intifada that began on September 29, 2000. Construction had ceased, alternative sources of employment inside Israel had dried up, and even the salaries of Palestinian civil servants were not being paid, or were only partially paid.

With almost every second Palestinian worker jobless, the gross national product of the PA dropped by 20 percent, whereas a 2 percent increase had been projected. Per capita income in the PA in 2000 was as low as $1,650. If Intifada continues, income would drop further, perhaps to $1,150 or less.

The 125,000 Palestinians that were denied access to work in Israel, after the Alaksa Intifada began in September 2000, in the past had earned enough money to support 7 others, or about 1 million people. The same could be said for the 115,000 police officers and government employees of the West Bank and Gaza Strip - while working and being paid, they were able to sustain nearly two thirds of the population.

Under the Oslo Agreement of 1993, Israel remained responsible for collecting income taxes from Palestinians working in Israel and for transferring those funds to the Palestinian Authority. Meanwhile, the Israeli government had been holding back these monies in response to the Intifada violence. More than $75 million was owed by Israel and remained unreleased by mid-March. Likewise, the PA owed money to the government of Israel for water, energy, and infrastructure. This reduced Israel's debt to the PA by millions of dollars.

The European Union meanwhile, delivered $25 million to the Palestinian Authority in December 2000. By February 2001, they had planned to convert loans worth $57 million into direct grants to the PA budget, but only as part of a broader international effort. Their foreign ministers called upon Israel to lift the border closures and resume paying the PA for tax revenues and customs on behalf of the Palestinian Authority.

The PA needed about $50 million a month to stay afloat. They borrowed $60 million from the international community to pay for February 2001 salaries. They were forced to transfer Arab pledges of $1 billion to tide them over for the rest of the year.

It appears, that even with rapid reversals in the economy of Palestinians, the three and a half million citizens of the bifurcated West Bank and Gaza Strip could be locked into a dependency, where outside government funding would be required to sustain daily life.

Chaos was fast approaching in the spring of 2002. The combined West Bank and Gaza economy, roughly one-20th the size of Israel's, was dependent on exporting goods sending day workers to Israel. The border closings and severe restrictions on movement inside the territories imposed by Israel during April and May, 2002 had doubled Palestinian poverty and unemployment rates. Relief officials had revised their figures--50 percent of Palestinians were then living below the poverty line and up to 60 percent were unemployed. A massive bailout response was demanded. Near stillborn, both fragile and destitute, the Palestinian Authority could be a welfare state in the future.

A MIDDLE EAST "MARSHALL PLAN" IS NEEDED.

President Bill Clinton, would never to be charged with insouciance on issues of peace in the Middle East. His Administration committed more than seven years to resolving this torturous conflict, indeed, to the very last days of his tenure in the White House.

President George W. Bush responded differently to the conflict from that of his predecessor, as is his Secretary of State, Colin Powell and other key advisors. His June 24, 2002 Presidential speech from the Rose Garden of the White House generated considerable hope. Along with the Saudi Peace Initiative and the UN's *Arab Development Report 2002*, the President has much to do to avert further strife and chaos.

RESETTLING AND COMPENSATING THE MILLIONS DISLOCATED

Refugees are people displaced during war. Palestinian refugees resulted from the War of Independence of 1948. They included Palestinians who lived within the Green Line. Jewish refugees were those ejected from Arab countries. Displaced persons are Palestinians displaced from the West Bank and Gaza Strip as a result of the 1967 war. Expired "Permit Palestinians" are former Palestinian residents who went abroad and overstayed their permits. As a result, they have not been allowed to reenter the territories. There are approximately 50,000 cases of expired permits, although Jordan claims 90,000.

The total of over 800,000 Jewish refugees from Arab countries (in 1948 there were 856,000 Jews in Arab countries, today there are 25,870 remaining) is almost identical to the 789,000 Arab-Palestinian refugees (539,000 in 1948 and 250,000 in 1967.) Jewish and Arab refugees were both settled in refugee camps.

A. *Palestinian refugees*

Many Palestinian refugees have demanded the right to return to their ancestral homes in Israel, buttressed by UN Resolution 194 (December 1948) (adopted at the 186th Plenary meeting) recommended under Section 11:

"Resolves that the refugees wishing to return to their homes and live at peace with their neighbors should be permitted to do so at the earliest practicable date, and the compensation should be paid of the property of those choosing not to return and for loss of or damage to property which, under principles of international law or inequity, should be made by the governments or authorities responsible."

696,000 Arabs lived within the 1948 Armistice Lines. 157,000 remained in their homes after the War of Independence, giving a net number of 539,000 Arabs who left Israel in 1948. Today, Palestinian refugees live in camps in some 60 locations in Gaza, the West Bank, Jordan, Syria, and Lebanon. Official statistics reveal there are 3,737,534 refugees registered with the UN Relief and Work Agency in Lebanon, Syria and Jordan, with an additional 90,000 in Iraq. Most are children and grandchildren of the original refugees.

Substantiated claims, could perhaps be paid for by the Middle East Recovery Program, will also be made for compensation for Palestinian refugees residing in non- West Bank-Gaza countries for as long as 52 years. For example, well over half of Jordan's population of 4.8 million is of Palestinian origin. The country plays host to 1.57 million registered refugees, slightly more than 40 percent of all Palestinians listed by the United Nations. Some 300,000 people live in 13 refugee camps throughout the Hashemite Kingdom of Jordan. Amman seeks the right of return to the PA and compensation for all refugees. Jordan's government seeks tens of billions of dollars in compensation for having hosted the refugees, claiming to spend $350 million annually to respond to their needs.

Israel's position does not recognize a "right," it does not recognize "responsibility," and it will not allow the return of refugees into its territory. According to Israel, in opposition to UN Security Council resolutions, the General Assembly resolutions have no binding international standings, but are merely recommendations. Sharon's first-government has attempted to dispel Palestinian hopes.

Israel urges resolving the refugee problem by resettling them in neighboring and "third" countries, which does not constitute a "return" to Israeli lands. (*Economist, The,* 2001, January 6).

B. *Israelis in the West Bank and Gaza Strip*

Underlying the entire issue is the PA's insistence that Israeli citizens leave their settlements in the Occupied Territories. Should those who had chosen to live in settlements within the

West Bank and Gaza Strip, now decide to leave, it will require large sums of money to enable a quick and comfortable exodus from areas of the Palestinian state. Their homes and other buildings should be maintained, not destroyed, for future use by Palestinian occupants.

C. *Jews from Arab countries*

In 1948, there were 740,000 to 856,000 Jews in Arab counties; by 1976, 97 percent were gone. 400,000 of these refugees entered Israel between 1948 and 1951, and a total of 586,268 had entered Israel by 1972.

It is difficult to determine, because records are old or non-existent, and proof is still complicated to uncover, that many of the Jews who left Arab nations to come to Israel, were unable to benefit from the sale of their properties, land, home, etc., before departure. In practically all of the Muslim countries in the Middle East and North Africa, Jews were forced to leave. They chose to move to Israel, where most lived for decades. They too, arguably, could make claims for restitution.

As funds might be used for assisting people who remained behind following the outbreak of war in 1948, monies could also be used to vastly improve the living conditions of all Israeli-Arabs. There are about 1 million living in the State of Israel. These Arabs, comprising about 18 percent of the country's population, have been deprived of their full rights and benefits as citizens of Israel. Following the war of independence in 1948, approximately 150,000 Palestinians remained within the boundaries of Israel following the war of independence in 1948. Their population has grown to about 1.2 million. They are poorly educated, receiving less than their share of government funds; they have an unemployment rate averaging at about 15 percent, twice that of the Jewish Israelis; only 5 percent of government jobs are allowed to be given to them; and as many as 60 percent of those working are employed by the Ministry of Health. Indeed, 95 percent are in the lowest socio-economic level within the State of Israel. (Levin).

Indeed, Israel ultimately intends to pursue compensation claims for tens of billions of U.S. dollars on behalf of 900,000 Jews who fled to Israel and elsewhere from Muslim lands in the aftermath of the establishment of the state and subsequent years, officials in the Israeli Justice Ministry say. The move is widely perceived of as an Israeli countermove, to be invoked in response to Palestinian claims for financial compensation under any formula for resolving the Palestinian refugees issue. (*Jerusalem Report, The*, 2002, December 16).

* * * * * * * * * * * * *

Time does not allow for delay; the luxury of waiting for conflict resolution has long passed. For the region, the advice given to Macbeth is sound: "If it were done when 'tis done, then 'twere well/It were done quickly" (specifically a message from Shakespeare and the people of the PA to President George W. Bush.)

The conflict in the Middle East has taken on different dimensions from those of more than a half-century ago when the State of Israel was restored:

(a) A population explosion is upon the region with few new employment opportunities predicted. According to World Bank estimates, the total population of MENA (defined as the Arab nations, Israel, Iran, and Turkey), will grow from 279.3 million in 1997, to reach 393.9 million in 2015, and to 481 million in 2030. Unevenly distributed, eight countries display population growth rates of well over 3 percent per annum. For example, Syria, which had a population of 8.7 million in 1980, was recently estimated to have a population of 17 million, and is expected to reach 28 million in 2030. Populations are getting younger. Contemporary Iran is a case in point. Two-thirds of a total of 69 million are already under 25 years.

(b) Neighboring nations, Egypt and Jordan now have peace treaties with Israel, while Syria and several others remain enemies of Israel. Consequently, hesitating until additional peace treaties are sealed is both unnecessary, shortsighted, and unproductive.

(c) In less than 15 years, the region is likely to explode over water disagreements, unless regional and long-range planning soon begins. Middle East leaders must agree on ways to conserve and share water, along with forging ahead to build desalination plants. Residents. of Amman, are permitted to turn on their water faucets just one day a week, and Jordan's population continues to increase. Syrians ration water, and its population is expected to double in 22 years. Palestinians are in a worse situation, and Israel, with its expected growth in population of 20 percent over the next decade has declining aquifers and shrinking rivers.

Unfortunately, the hard facts of life replace optimism for those living in the West Bank, Gaza Strip and other countries with large Palestinian refugee populations. Since Oslo of 1993, unemployment is higher, wages are down, and probably most humiliating and frustrating is that the promise for a better life does not appear to be within reach. Hopelessness has replaced hope.

No wonder the West Bank and Gaza are reliant on Israel, which continues as its main market, its source for imports, and its export route. At the same time, Israel is obligated to reimburse the Palestinian Authority for taxes, health coverage, and social security payments taken from her citizens who have worked and continue to work in Israel. This dependency is a direct clash with any ideology hoping for Palestinian sovereignty.

A BINDING ECONOMIC COMMITMENT TO THE PALESTINIANS

Lost in the twirl of events is the binding historic April 29, 1994 *Paris Economic Agreement* which took over six months of arduous Israeli-Palestinian economic talks to negotiate. This accord granted Palestinian economic independence and cemented the two economies. The final agreement ensured the free movement of goods into Israel except for five items on which quotas were imposed for five years. In addition, Palestinian restrictions were lifted on exports to other markets. (Rosenberg, 1997, pp. 311-312).

More importantly for the Palestinian Authority, this agreement was to bring about a substantial lowering of their longstanding trade deficit with Israel by providing them with virtually free access to Israel's markets, and by allowing them to. purchase goods from other cheaper suppliers outside of Israel.

This economic accord provided for free trade and the establishment of a limited form of customs union, initially between Israel and the autonomous areas of Gaza and Jericho, that was extended to the rest of the West Bank. Exceptions included industrial inputs, durable goods and basic food products from Arab countries, basic food products from other Islamic nations, and basic industrial and agricultural machinery from all countries.

TO THE FUTURE

The proposed Middle East Recovery Program (MERP) would hasten further implementation of the Paris Economic Agreement and would move cross-border regional economic integration into an interdependence of contiguous nations by encouraging, over time, the creation of JIPTA - the Jordanian-Israeli-Palestinian (Free) Trade Agreement. JIPTA argues against fences and closures, and would work to reduce and ultimately eliminate tariffs and quotas to forge an open trading community of capital, goods, and services between the three entities. In essence, JIPTA would someday bear witness to the fruits of the Middle East Recovery Program with tariff-lowering and the increase of tariff-free imports and exports, all in pursuit of employment, higher living standards, and stability for people of the region.

As a precursor to JIPTA, the Middle East Recovery Program would encourage the negotiation of Trade and Investment Framework Agreements (TIFAs) that would help set a structure for improving the trade and investment regimes of countries within the region. A TIFA would offer a platform from which to address specific trade and investment barriers and contribute to improving trade and investment policies along internationally-accepted standards. As such, TIFAs are a critical component of promoting closer trade relations in the Middle East and beyond.

With success on the horizon, the Middle East Recovery Program would eventually promote interaction and expansion to other nations of the region, such as Egypt, Lebanon and those of North Africa to incorporate other Arab countries into a Middle East/North Africa Economic Community of 300 million people. The model could someday, also be expanded to include non-Arab-Muslim nations from Central Asia, plus Afghanistan, Pakistan, and perhaps Turkey thereby evolving an ascending 28-nation potential economic powerhouse - a Middle East/North Africa/Central Asia Community (MENACA).

Just as the Marshall Plan led the way for economic prosperity of the eventual 15-nation European Union (and growing), where its 375 million citizens, free from the burden and disaster of war consume ¼ of all world goods, the Middle East Recovery Program, with an aid package of many billions of dollars, would likewise be a historical pivotal decision for bringing stability and prosperity to a region that has suffered far too long.

A redefined Middle East can one day cover territories from North Africa, into the traditional Middle East, and beyond to include the additional 8 nations from Central Asia, Pakistan, Afghanistan, and possibly Turkey. A population totaling one-half a billion people now defines this greater neighborhood. The newly extended boundary for deliberation and impact, might include as many as 28 nations, all an outgrowth of the original three of the Middle East Community- the Israelis, Palestinians, and Jordanians.

MERP is about the 21st century and modernization, dedicated to future promise and successes in civil-societies, perhaps the ultimate variable needed for implementation.

CHAPTER III

THE MARSHALL PLAN

"A working economy has to be revived to permit the emergence of political and social conditions in which free institutions can exist. "

George C. Marshall

Before the world became fixated on the phrase "nation building" the more familiar way to describe this event was "reconstruction accompanied by financial assistance." Certainly, the 1948 Marshall Plan became the model for this gesture of humanitarian excellence.

The desultory conditions of the post World War II period, with its cold war, devastation, economic disarray, national mistrust, containment of former enemies, and Soviet threats from beyond the borders of Western Europe has been well documented. Forces of the day that both supported and fought the Marshall Plan's passage and the involved personalities are described below. Finally, there is a comparison of the major issues of the Marshall Plan with those of the proposed Middle East Recovery Program.

McCullough notes (pp. 618-619) that one of the ironies of history is that President Truman became the first world leader to recognize Israeli statehood six months after passage of the Marshall Plan, on May 14, 1948. Truman did this despite advice to the contrary from Secretary of State Marshall, who warned that support for a Jewish nation would incite the Arabs, risk compromising America's oil supply, and possibly give the Soviets an opportunity to expand their sphere of influence.

Between the end of the World War in 1945 and 1947, the United States had already loaned or given nearly $6 billion to save the starving and unemployed in Europe; both for friend and former foe. President Harry Truman repeatedly argued that any country that had avoided physical damage its land during the war was obligated to come to the assistance of needy countries. Relief was welcomed, moreover the answer was that outright funding was required for reconstruction.

A key figure in Marshall's State Department, Undersecretary of State for Economic Affairs, Will Clayton, was a former business executive. He was convinced that the balance of payments between countries was a pretty reliable guide to the depth of financial trouble of each country after the war. He calculated that $5 billion annually, over a five-year period would get Europe's economy jumpstarted to a self-supporting level. Upon returning from a fact-finding European mission, Clayton found life far worse than he had anticipated and reported this to both Truman and Marshall. (Pogue, pp. 221-222).

In 1948, three years following the end of the war, Congress approved funds for the European Recovery Program. Claiming that it would not pass Congress were it to be named for himself, President Truman insisted that it be called the Marshall Plan, named for his Secretary of State George C. Marshall, regarded by many as the "greatest living American." (Bernstein, p. 236).

After the disastrous winter of 1946-47, Marshall knew that Germany, as the future economic engine of Europe had to be revitalized, or there might well be no European recovery at all. (Pogue, p. 207). Far worse than expected, the devastation, unemployment, malnutrition, and starvation, especially in West Germany demanded large-scale aid. Indeed, some obfuscated allied-European leaders protested the offer to their former enemy, but Marshall insisted that without Germany's resurgence, European recovery would only be a dream.

He found the European situation in a process of disintegration "which would quickly permit the development of a police state regime." (p. 208). Eventually 17 nations participated. "In all the history of the world," President Harry Truman wrote soon after passage of the Marshall Plan, "we are the first great nation to feed and support the conquered." (McCullough, p. 583).

Without Truman's determination to share American bounty with war-stricken citizens of Europe,, the European Recovery Program would not have gone forward to Congress. The President was committed to spread "the faith" (p. 555) of freedom and democracy, and was convinced that the stricken nations of Europe needed everything and could afford to purchase nothing, "We are the giant of the economic world. Whether we like it or not, the future pattern of economic relations depends upon us." (p.556).

The U.S. Administration received ammunition from international sources to support its position for this package. Winston Churchill emphasized the plight of Europe, "It is a rubble-heap, a charnel house, a breeding ground of pestilence and hate." (Phillips, p. 181).

At that time, this aid package, was the largest U.S. grant in American history - was approved at nearly $17 billion. This donation by the American people contributed significantly to European stability and economic rehabilitation, and ultimately to the creation of the European Economic Community, later renamed the European Union. In the end, only $13 billion, $88 billion in today's dollars, was actually spent.

Marshall introduced the world to this historic aid plan on June 5, 1947 during a commencement speech at Harvard University, "Our policy is directed not against any country or doctrine, but against hunger, poverty, desperation and chaos. Its purpose should be the revival of a working economy in the world so as to permit the emergence of political and social conditions in which free institutions can exist" (Pogue, p. 198). The goal was to revive agriculture and trade so that stricken nations might be self-supporting.

Secretary of State Marshall reached out to the Soviet Union as well as European nations to work together in creating an action that would serve their needs, not that of the United States, "It would be neither fitting nor efficacious for this Government to undertake to draw up unilaterally a program designed to place Europe on its feet economically. That is the business of the Europeans. The initiative, I think, must come from Europe. The role should consist of friendly aid in the drafting of a European plan, and of later support for such a program so far as it is practical for us to do so. The arrangement should be a joint one, agreed to by a number, if not all, European nations." (p. 218).

Throughout 1947, the U.S. State Department became increasingly aware of and concerned about Europe's economic collapse. A once-hoped- for rapid recovery after the war had not materialized. Undersecretary Dean Acheson, who later replaced Marshall as Secretary of State, warned that "America might have to support the reconstruction of Europe." The Policy Planning Staff, created by Marshall to be the new think-tank of the Department was quick to respond. (p. 254).

The State Department and the State-War-Navy group had filed reports on the conditions in Europe--the latter report was ninety-three pages long. The news was dismal. "Disintegrating forces are becoming evident," (p. 224) reported Marshall on national radio.

In late May, William L. Clayton wrote a gloomy message to Marshall, "It is now obvious that we have grossly underestimated the destruction to the European economy by the war." (p. 231). He urged a grant of "six to seven billion dollars worth of goods a year for three years." (p. 232). As the former head of the world's largest cotton brokerage, far from being altruistic, he envisioned huge markets for the U.S. that would sell products across the Atlantic. (Clayton also recommended a European economic federation nearly ten years before the European common market was created.)

It was time to commence the process of confidence-building and outreach. The U.S. determined that Europe must lead the way with recommendations, information, and calls for assistance, each having to be supported with accurate evidence. On June 12, 1947, U.S. diplomatic mission representatives commenced surveys in countries to which they were assigned to determine:

. the current economic situation and the immediate help needed;
. the seriousness of the economic situation for the coming year;
. whether matters would improve with the exchange of goods with other countries of Western and Central Europe;
. the obstacles to overcome;
. the extent of contribution each country could make to general European rehabilitation; and
- the degree of Soviet or Communist pressure likely to inhibit the country's initiative and cooperation in a recovery program.

At times on the defensive, always tuned to the political swings of the day, the U.S. State Department demanded to know (1) why was European recovery proceeding so slowly; (2) what could Europe do to help itself; and (3) with minimum aid from the United States, how long would it take Europe to get back on its feet?

Concern that some European governments might resist U.S. involvement (there was considerable wrangling and

positioning, especially among the leaders of France, the U.K. and
the Soviet Union,) Ernest Bevin, Foreign Minister of the United
Kingdom "warmly welcomed" the Marshall Plan proposal. (pp.
232-33). His encomium for Marshall's approach was visionary.
He considered the Secretary of State's address of the greatest
historic importance and upheld the General's belief that Europe
should be responsible for the next move.

Upon learning of Marshall's speech, Bevin stated "I
assure you, gentlemen, it was like a lifeline to sinking men. It
seemed to bring hope where there was none. The generosity of it
was beyond my belief."

Bevin compared the position of the U.S. with that of
Britain following the Napoleonic wars. He found a precedent for
America's aid, in both money and goods. At that time, Britain
possessed 30 percent of the world's wealth, while in 1947 the
United States held half. After the Napoleonic conflicts, the British
had practically given away their exports for nearly eighteen years,
resulting in one hundred years of stability on the Continent. (p.
220).

Emotions ran deep when it came to assisting a former
enemy. The issue of supporting Germany remained in the
forefront of the debate. The French wanting a weak Germany.
England, worried that a weak Germany meant the continued
support of her shattered economy, feared that the Marshall Plan
would favor German reconstruction over theirs. The United States
argued that the economic calamity of the Germans was far worse
than that of France, and with its population of 66 million citizens,
Germany must be included to have a major impact on the future
of Europe. (p. 223).

Following analysis of overseas data, the initial report was
approved on September 12, 1947 by representatives of Austria,
Belgium, Denmark, Ireland, France, Greece, Iceland, Italy,
Luxembourg, the Netherlands, Norway, Portugal, Sweden,
Switzerland, Turkey, and the United Kingdom. It was rushed by
Marshall to the President for consideration. "It is easy to propose

a great plan, but exceedingly difficult to manage the form and procedure so that it has a fair chance of political survival." (p. 223).

Realizing the potential crushing defeat before a Congress that was in no mood to approve large, self-perpetuating projects, Marshall presented a restricted four-year program as promoting economic recovery in the sixteen participating nations and West Germany by:
. making strong efforts to restore agricultural production levels to prewar standards, and industrial production to somewhat higher totals than those established immediately before the outbreak of the war;
. creating and maintaining stable internal economic conditions;
. establishing and continuing an organization to promote and increase economic cooperation among the countries involved; and
. undertaking to solve the dollar deficit in each country through expansion of exports.

Initially, it was assumed that the required sum would amount to $22 billion, (at one time estimated by the Europeans to approach $29 billion) but under pressure, especially from Congress, the amount was scaled down to a final $17 billion before it was formally presented. (In the end, only $13 billion was spent.) (McCullough, p. 579).

Marshall and the President devoted considerable energies to convince Congress that the recovery plan was affordable. It wasn't easy. The Republicans by 1947 were determined to reduce taxes and expenditures following the great costs of the war. Under attack for what some considered wasteful was the $3.25 billion in foreign relief that had already been loaned to the United Kingdom. That was before Marshall came forward for further funding.

Praise was forthcoming from the Europe. Europeans felt that the initiative taken by Marshall was the most important single step that any government had taken since the end of the war. Fearing Congress would only support temporary relief rather than full recovery, members of a European mission argued that if they achieved only partial relief, "Europe had gone so far downhill that full recovery would not be possible... The forging of the recovery of Western Europe can only be done once and it has to be done now." (Pogue, pp. 239-240).

There was considerable muscle flexing and arm twisting required to secure approval. It was already seven months since Marshall's Harvard University address and there was some concern that the drawn-out process was causing a loss in interest. In testimony before the House Foreign Affairs Committee, he knew that he had to intone the same warnings again and again: "....so long as hunger, poverty, desperation, and resulting chaos threaten the great concentrations of people in Western Europe-some 270 million-there will surely develop social unease and political consequences on every side." (p. 240).

Congress reviewed reports from sixteen countries that, for the first time in history, had collectively outlined their economic contributions and facilities and described measures that would be needed by all.

To institutionalize the Plan over a four-and-a-half year period was of great and proper concern to the House Foreign Affairs Committee. Marshall believed that there should be an executive agency run by one person "fitted into the existing machinery of government." (p. 242). He wanted the organization to be named the Economic Cooperation Administration to related to the nation's foreign policy without being controlled by the Secretary of State. (p. 255).

Congress had different ideas which were ultimately accepted. They wanted a man with an industrial background to head the Administration, a person with impressive business credential without diplomacy. President Truman would make the appointment. He initially wanted to have Dean Acheson, then back in private law practice, to become ECA's first administrator. (Phillips, p. 179). Acheson convinced the President to look elsewhere as he felt the Republicans would reject his name during an election year. Truman did finally nominate Acheson, but the Senate would not confirm him.

On April 5, 1948, the name of Paul Hoffman, (Pogue, p. 255) a Republican, President of the Studebaker Corporation, and Chairman of the Committee on Economic Development was submitted and approved by the Senate. Once Hoffman was appointed, Marshall left its operation to this talented executive who said, "He never made a suggestion on appointing anyone, never made a suggestion on how to run the show. I kept him informed because he was Secretary of State, but I think his feeling was that as long as it was going all right, that was it...we never had any differences ourselves" (p. 255).

Often referred to in the sweep of economic diplomacy, where the expansion of trade was a U.S. strategy, the following sentiment was aired. "Dollars," according to Frenchman, Raymond Aron, (p. 31) "were indubitably used as a weapon against Communism and as an instrument in the policy of containment."

The Soviet Union, though invited to participate in the Marshall Plan, soon withdrew from negotiations with other major European powers and also prevented its satellites from joining the program. Czechoslovakia, which had indicated strong interest, yielded to Russian pressure and retreated. To this day there remains a mystery as to why Generalissimo Stalin rejected the U.S. offer of financial help. (Pogue, p. 226). Was it suspicion of American motives in view of the earlier requests for loans, or a resistance by the U.S. for a list of requirements for multilateral relations? The Marshall Plan, designed to transcend the Cold War, became an extension of containment following the Soviet Union's rejection, thus virtually assuring that Congress would approve the Administration's request.

Hints of disapproval were expressed. *Pravda, Ukraine* newspaper (pp. 219-220) led the charge against, what they referred to as Marshall Doctrine, in an attempt to obfuscate the situation, "evidence of even wider plans of America, of a new stage in Washington's campaign against forces of world democracy and progress.. Marshall proposes or rather demands quick formation of (a) notorious western bloc but under conditional and absolute leadership of American imperialism.....From retail purchase of several European countries, Washington has conceived design of the wholesale purchase of the whole European continent."

On July 2, 1947, Soviet Foreign Minister Molotov explained some of the nation's objections to the Marshall Plan: "It would lead to interference in the internal affairs of European countries, particularly those which have the greatest need for outside aid, this can only complicate relations between the countries of Europe and hamper their cooperation...." (pp. 223-224).

Then, on October 5, 1947, the formal Communist communique condemned the program as only: "a farce, a European branch of the general world plan of political expansion being realized by the United States of America in all parts of the world.....The aggressors of yesterday--the capitalist tycoons of Germany and Japan--are being prepared by the United States of America for a new role, as tools of the imperialistic policy in Europe and Asia of the United States of America.......In these conditions, the anti-imperialist democratic camp has to close its ranks....and work out its tactics against the chief forces of the imperialist camp." (p. 228). (Most experts, then and now, believe that had the Soviet Union accepted the invitation, Congress certainly would have defeated the European Recovery Program initiative.)

Communist aggression was never spoken of in Marshall's Harvard speech, but he knew that its mention would overcome resistance to funding a program for reconstruction, and he warned once again that the nation had to accept the consequences that a collapse could end in a dictatorship of police states.

Marshall's campaign to win approval became more forceful as weeks passed. Speaking at the University of California in Berkeley, he talked of "a world-wide struggle between freedom and tyranny, between the self-rule of the many as opposed to the dictatorship of the ruthless few." (p. 239).

The Chairman of the Committee asked whether the ideology in the U.S. offer of aid would not be seen as a form of American imperialism attempting to overpower the sovereignty of nations. Marshall responded that were the U.S. engaged in such a conspiracy of economic imperialism, we would need to "have a basis of a more Machiavellian approach than is exhibited here with public hearings and public discussions on every side with regard to every issue." (p. 241).

President Truman acted quickly. On October 23, 1947, he called Congress into a session to commence debate on November 17th. Marshall would be present at the joint meeting of the Senate Foreign Relations Committee and the House Foreign Affairs Committee to outline reasons for interim aid as a part of the larger, long-range program. His peroration was decisive.

Writing to his wife, Bess, President Truman told how preoccupied he was with the immense projected cost of the Marshall Plan..."If it works out as planned it will cost us about $16 billion over a four-year period......just the amount of the national debt when Franklin (Roosevelt) took over. He ran it up to 40 odd and then the war came along and it is 257...." Several days later, he told her "Our war cost that year (1945) was set at 105 billion. The 16.5 is for a four-year period and is for *peace*. A Russian war would cost us 400 billion and untold lives, most civilian. So I must do what I can." (McCullough, p. 579).

The President pressed forward and addressed the joint session of Congress on November 17th, proposing short-term aid of $597 million to cover needs until the end of March 1948.

Truman would ask Congress for the Marshall Plan on December 19th, The next few years can determine whether the free countries of Europe will be able to preserve their heritage of freedom. If Europe fails to recover, the peoples of these countries might be driven to the philosophy of despair--the philosophy which contends that their basic wants can be met only by the surrender of their basic rights to totalitarian control. (p. 582) Congress, in turn, passed an interim aid bill to carry Western Europe through the winter.

The President was so convinced of Marshall's influence with the public and his outstanding leadership in preparing the way for passage of the ERP that he began to refer to the measures as the "Marshall Plan." (The January 5, 1948 cover of *Time* Magazine had the caption "Hope for those that need it" as Marshall was declared "Man of the Year" for a second time. The first time was in 1944 when he was General of the Army.) (Pogue, p. 237).

Increasingly, Congressional opposition to the Marshall Plan was rooted in the fear that the U.S. economy could not bear the financial burden and that American funds were being poured into the "rat holes" of Europe. At another moment of suspicion, Congressman Hubert Ellis of West Virginia, addressing the House, insisted that now was the time to resist Marshall's program by yelling "Stop, thief; police...A bankrupt and demoralized America can make no contribution to the suffering of the world." (Bernstein, p. 265).

In September 1947, the President made public the three economic studies he had ordered, each of which concluded that the United States was capable and obligated by self-interest to make a massive effort for Europe's reconstruction.

There was opposition to its passage, even from the most unexpected quarters. Loy W. Henderson, head of the Office of Near Eastern Affairs of the State Department worried about the consequences of the Marshall Plan should Arab oil be severed. Europe was dependent on Arab states for 80 percent of its oil so that the formation of a Jewish State, he stressed to the Secretary of State, could be disastrous to the long-range interests of the United States. (Phillips, p. 168). (For similar reasons, both Secretaries of State Marshall and his successor Dean Acheson opposed Truman's desire to support the creation of the State of Israel.)

Marshall, though sensitive to Washington pressures, remained firm. Taking the stand before the Senate Foreign Relations Committee on the proposed European Recovery Program, he, in his usual calm fashion, assured the panel and the nation, "This program will cost our country billions of dollars. It will impose a burden on the American taxpayer. It will require sacrifices today in order that we may enjoy security and peace tomorrow." (Pogue, p. 249).

Early into 1948, the Department of State presented the Bill to Congress. The big battle was fought in the Senate where some thought the amount requested was too great. Opponents wanted to slash the amount and reduce the time from fifteen months to twelve.

Senator Vandenberg's support and voice was essential. As the closing of debate approached, he urged that the U.S. accept greater responsibilities of leadership. He employed the Soviet threat effectively. (p. 238). Following two weeks of argument, thirty-eight Democrats were joined by thirty-one Republicans to pass the Economic Cooperation Act by a vote of 69-17 at five minutes past midnight on March 14, 1948. Then the fight would turn to the House of Representatives.

On March 31st, the House accepted most of the Senate's version, shouting the Bill through in a voice vote of 329 to 74. It authorized economic aid of $5.3 billion ($4.3 billion in appropriations and $1 billion in flexible credit,) for Europe for a 12-month period. The Marshall Plan was about 12 percent of the entire federal budget, and 2 percent of U.S. GNP. Between 1948 and 1951, some $13.5 billion was distributed. (McCullough, pp. 532-533).

For three years, Western Europe required U.S. help. Clark Clifford recalled, "I think it is one of the proudest moments in American history. What happened during that period was that Harry Truman and the United States saved the free world." (p.

564). Dean Acheson described it more biblically, as being "present at the creation." (Pogue, p. 202).

*   *   *   *   *   *   *   *   *   *   *   *   *   *

Known officially as the Foreign Assistance Act of 1948, (Foreign Assistance Act, April 3, 1948) the Findings approved of "…..a plan of European recovery, open to all such nations which cooperate in such plan, based upon a strong production effort, the expansion of foreign trade, the creation and maintenance of internal financial stability, and the development of economic cooperation, including all possible steps to establish and maintain equitable rates of exchange and to bring about the progressive elimination of trade barriers."

Entered as Chapter 169-Public Law 472, it begins with a statement of principle "An Act to promote world peace and the general welfare, national interest, and foreign policy of the United States, through economic, financial, and other measures necessary to the maintenance of conditions abroad in which free institutions may survive and consistent with the maintenance of the strength and stability of the United States."

The Act's Declaration of Policy concluded:

Provided, That no assistance to the participating countries herein contemplated shall seriously impair the economic stability of the United States. It is further declared to be the policy of the United States that continuity of assistance provided by the United States should, at all times, be dependent upon continuity of cooperation among countries participating in the program. In brief, President Truman (McCullough, p. 583) called for (1) authorization for the expenditure of $17 billion in support of European recovery from April 1, 1948 to June 30, 1952; (2) an immediate appropriation of $6.8 billion to carry the program for its first fifteen months, from April 1, 1948 to June 30, 1949; and (3) authorization to create an Economic Cooperation Administration, an independent agency answerable to the President, to administer the program. I know that the Congress will, as it should, consider with great care the legislation necessary to put the program into effect. (p. 583) This consideration should proceed as rapidly as possible in order that the program may become effective by April 1, 1948. It is for this reason that I am presenting my recommendations to the Congress now, rather than awaiting its reconvening in January...I recommend this program.. in full confidence of its wisdom and necessity as a major step in our nation's quest for a just and lasting peace. (p. 583).

To help administer the Plan, the Organization for European Economic Cooperation (OEEC) was set up, eventually consisting of eighteen European nations including West Germany, together with the United States and Canada. In the early years, the Marshall Plan dollars crossed the ocean to provide European participants with the foreign exchange they needed to buy more goods abroad than they could have traded with their exports.

Before the Act terminated, U.S. support for war-torn Europe (pre- Marshall Plan and resulting from the Marshall Plan) ultimately totaled $19,541,000 in economic assistance (82 percent in grants). In 1951, the Plan's implementation was transferred to the Mutual Security Program, which continued to operate until 1956. In 1961, the OEEC was superseded by the Paris-based Organization for Economic Cooperation and Development.

Within two weeks of Congress' approving the appropriation for European Recovery, the freighter *John H. Quick* sailed out of Galveston, Texas with 9,000 tons of purchased wheat, the first cargo of the Marshall Plan. Truman wrote privately after approval "In all the history of the world, we are the first great nation to feed and support the conquered...." (McCullough, p. 583). The United States had never appeared so great or so generous.

Greece and Turkey were subsequently incorporated into the European Recovery Program. The Marshall Plan cost the U.S. taxpayer less than originally expected. More importantly, it did save free and independent governments in Western Europe; it did put Europe on the road to a booming industrial prosperity; and it did pave the way for European economic integration.

In December 1951, the Economic Cooperation Administration closed its doors. (Pogue, p.256). The Marshall Plan was for all intents and purposes now over. The closure was the result of conservative critics in Congress and of the shift in Presidential strategy from economic assistance to military aid and rearmament. Economic diplomacy, as practiced by Secretary Marshall, was to be a thing of the past.

1997, celebrating the fiftieth anniversary of the European Recovery Program, Germany's Helmut Schmidt said: "The United States ought not to forget that the emerging European Union is one of its own great achievements; it would never have happened without the Marshall Plan." The twists and turns bring new dreams and opportunities. Let's hope that future leaders of the world will say the same for the copycat - Middle East Recovery Program--the greatest tribute to the 1948 Marshall Plan. (*Economist, The*, 1997, January 5).

THE McCARTHY ATTACKS

When the American public protests government policy and policy makers, most citizens find it worthy--an act reflecting cherished democratic principles. On the other hand, they are often unnerved when one of their few elected officials dedicates his or her career to vindictive attacks on national heroes, past and present.

Several books written about Senator Joseph R. McCarthy included McCarthy's harsh and belligerent treatment of George C. Marshall. The books are worth reading, but this intent for the section of this book, is to   suggest the possibility of a repeat performance from the floor of the U.S. Congress, from other chambers of power, and from the streets of America when it is time to take a position on the Middle East Recovery Program. These kinds of behind-the-scene events reveal humanity's struggle.

A new generation will have to carry the torch from 1947's Marshall Plan into the new century. The lessons to be learned reveal not only what was, but most importantly, what might be in the Middle East, North Africa, Central Asia, and beyond.

Years after the Marshall Plan was implemented, sufficient proof were available that the Plan not only enabled Western Europe to get back on its feet, to embrace a future with dignity and to fulfill a promise of economic integration. It also kept the Soviet Union at bay and her soldiers away from Europe's borders.

Many praised Marshall for his role in proposing, supporting, and gaining legislative approval for the European Recovery Program which was instrumental in rebuilding war-torn Europe. "There are few men whose qualities of mind and character have impressed me so greatly as those of General Marshall," wrote England's Prime Minister Winston S. Churchill. "He is a great American, but he is far more than that...He has always fought vigorously against defeatism, discouragement and disillusion. Succeeding generations must not be allowed to forget his achievements and his example." (Pogue, p. 502)

During the period of anti-Communist hysteria in the United States, the attacks on President Truman, General Marshall and the Marshall Plan persisted. None were more aggressive than the prolonged assault by U.S. Senator Joseph McCarthy. Favoring General Douglas MacArthur as "the greatest American that was ever born," McCarthy undertook the destruction of MacArthur's most formidable adversary-Marshall. (Reeves, p. 370).

McCarthy, the elfin-like, junior Senator from Wisconsin, and in his determination to obfuscate and prove that the Soviet Union was planning to take over the world, decided anyone was fair target for him. In his short Congressional, and stormy career, he brought down some of the country's most celebrated people. His swinging treason charges, like sledgehammers, brought himself down in the end.

McCarthy accused the wartime Chief of Staff Marshall of conspiring with those who wished to see the Communists inherit the earth. On June 15, 1951, he went to the Senate with a briefcase full of manuscripts that would, he stated, be useful to the Senate Armed Services and Foreign Relations Committee. It was, according to Richard Rovere, (p. 171) "the most daring and seditious of McCarthy's actions. It stands today as the most famous of his speeches, and yet it is,....a speech to which no one ever listened and which very few have ever read."

McCarthy stood on the Senate floor and delivered a small portion of his scathing 60,000 word speech against George C. Marshall and his plan of economic aid for Europe. He stopped speaking after reading about one-third of this talk (by then most of the Senators had walked out of the Chamber) and stated that the portion he had just completed and the remaining unread text - all of its 48 pages would appear in the U.S. Congressional Record.   Later it was published as a book - "America's Retreat from Victory." (At another time, McCarthy would accuse General Dwight D. Eisenhower of joining, part and parcel, in Marshall's "traitorous" scheme.)

"I think it is clear that, in these great matters of life and death," bellowed the Senator, "President Truman is in the custody of Marshall."

Continuing, McCarthy said that General Marshall was a man "whose every important act for years has contributed to the prosperity of the enemy." (Anderson, pp. 356-357).

Anderson claimed (p. 357) that McCarthy would blame both President Harry Truman and George C. Marshall, who was the first Administration's Secretary of State, and later Secretary of Defense, for the loss in the free world of 100 million people a year to international Communism.

Although McCarthy stopped short of uttering treason, he declared that Marshall's career was "steeped in falsehood and that when his story is fully told it would be of a conspiracy so black that its principals shall be forever deserving of the malediction of all honest men." (Reeves, p. 436).

Time Magazine reported: "In familiar fashion, McCarthy twisted quotes, drew unwarranted conclusions from the facts he did get right, (and) accused Marshall of having made common cause with Stalin since 1943." (Anderson, p. 278).

In 1953, the Nobel Peace Prize was awarded to George C. Marshall, not as soldier, but as statesman and humanitarian for his sponsorship of the European Recovery Program.

Marshall's speech before a glittering audience at Oslo University's Festival Hall included his insightful vision of the Western world's future challenge: "We must present democracy as a force holding within itself the seeds of unlimited progress by the human race. By our actions we should make it clear that such a democracy is a means to a better way of life, together with a better understanding of nations. Tyranny inevitably must retire before the tremendous moral strength of the gospel of freedom and self-respect for the individual, but we have to recognize that these democratic principles do not flourish on empty stomachs and that people turn to false promises of dictators because they are hopeless and anything promises something better than the miserable existence that they endure."

Marshall's words augured well for the plight of post World War II's citizens. His words can be advanced 55 years, and the same phrases reach out to the people of the Middle East Recovery Program that hope indeed burns eternal.

Likewise, the proposed Middle East Recovery Program will survive the attacks on its concepts and organization. Indeed, times are different; this is not 1947. The Soviet Union no longer exists as it once did, and the fear of communism has all but disappeared. Yet, new threats are on stage. The United States needs a plan that will not only defeat future terrorism and biological/chemical attacks, but will work with welcoming nations to reform their dysfunctioning, current forms of governance.

MERP funds can be used to encourage the movement towards moderation, for governments to reform, become more transparent, and aim to gain legitimacy. Some of these monies will be used for education, to show that Islam is compatible with modern society, open to men and women, open to all faiths, open to differing ideas, cultures, and ideologies. Today's politics will witness onslaughts from the region and elsewhere. Indeed, every generation yields its own challenges.

Marshall's portrait is an imposing fixture in Colin Powell's Washington office. The example of McCarthy's attacks on General George C. Marshall is a sharp message for the Secretary of State and other officials that it might be replayed again and again.

There will assuredly be a struggle for the minds, hearts, and purses of the American people when the debate over funding the Middle East Recovery Program commences. Congressional leaders at that time will take positions on the pros and cons of the revisited Marshall Plan concept; will juggle the tradeoff of costs vs. benefits to national security; will appease some constituents at the same time that they antagonize others; and will determine MERP's destiny.

There will likely be attempts to sabotage the proposed MERP by zealots within the United States and beyond her borders. Ultimately, the pluses, when listened to with passion and understanding, should be embraced as an affordable cost for lasting stability and prosperity throughout the Middle East region.

Americans won't ever forget that arguably the most powerful nation in the history of mankind, was shaken and could have been brought to its knees on September 11, 2001 by a highly motivated, 18-man operation wielding low-tech devices and high resolve to turn American power on itself.

There remains a significant part of the world's population that remains angry with the United States. The U.S. government must develop long term plans to strengthen relationships with many of the world's citizens who remain both hungry and disenfranchised, and who feel the sting and injustices of violence, hate, corruption and hopelessness. Indeed, they may feel there is little for which to live.

The Marshall Plan of 1948 helped to rebuild a devastated Europe; it also ensured U.S. security throughout the remaining 20th century. A Middle East Recovery Program can offset a world in peril replaced with global order.

THE MARSHALL PLAN (MP) and THE MIDDLE EAST RECOVERY PROGRAM (MERP) - A COMPARISON
There are appropriate similarities and differences that can be made by contrasting the suggested *Middle East Recovery Program (MERP)* concept with that of the European Recovery Program-*The Marshall Plan (MP)*.

MP: On April 29, 1947, then U.S. Secretary of State George C. Marshall summoned to his office George F. Kennan, a key participant on the Policy Planning Staff on European aid. He stated that "Europe is in a mess...Something will have to be done." (Pogue, p. 555).
MERP: Today, the Middle East, North Africa and Central Asia region is a "mess"....Something will have to be done. The U.S.'s past policies must be re-examined and replaced with new ones.

MP: Speaking in a nationwide radio address, Marshall warned: "The patient is sinking while the doctors deliberate." (p. 558)
MERP: September 28th, 2000 commenced Intifada II violence. Its continuation is evidence of the lack of closure, of the inadequate movement towards resolution of the Middle East conflict. Meetings without movement leave the Israeli-Palestinian contest in shambles. Cures by trading are insufficient; a thrust forward is needed before time runs out, and before a bomb replaces the stalemate.

While North Africa appears momentarily stable, Central Asia and its immediate neighborhood is misunderstood and sinking in poverty, drought, and extremism.

MP: The Marshall Plan not only encouraged, but even forced Western European countries to think together, not separately, about recovery programs.

MERP: Nationalism throughout the Middle East region is changing. Today, organizations are essential to stand about the nation-state for the sake of stability. The institutions have become the vehicle for open communication, transparency and placement of common problems before participants.

MP: Marshall said: "It was my feeling that the Soviets were doing everything possible to achieve a complete breakdown in Europe...." And later "that is, they were doing anything they could to create greater turbulence. The major problem was how to counter this negative Soviet policy and restore the European economy." (p. 251).

MERP: Regional extremists, such as those evidenced by Osama bin Laden and the Taliban organization and ongoing fundamentalists, Saddam Hussein, historical enemies of Israel and western society continue to call for the elimination of the State of Israel, perhaps even the elimination of Europe and the United States. How to deal with global terrorism and biological/chemical attacks, while rejuvenating collapsing nations is a complex and difficult, but necessary, task.

MP: Kennan believed that the Communists would portray U.S. aid as a "sinister effort to further American hegemony onto the people of Western Europe." (p. 304).

MERP: Anti-Israeli governments will continue their attack against Israel, as will other potent groups who talk of yet another U.S. plot to control their destiny, and oil supplies, and those of other Arab/Muslim and non-Arab/Muslim cultures and nations. U.S. economic clout, though a force of significance, will be no match for political wisdom; the economic clout, remains available as the glue to sustain a positive movement towards stability and prosperity.

MP: The Planning Staff on European aid recommended to Marshall: "To avoid Communist interference..suggested that U.S. assistance depend on guarantees from those European countries seeking aid that any assistance would not be misused or sabotaged by Communists." (p. 227).

MERP: The same approach must be displayed in making certain that pro-extremist groups/nations that seek aid would guarantee that they will not utilize the monies for subversive efforts.

MP: Anticipating the future European Economic Community, the Planning Staff on European aid urged encouragement of some form of "regional political association of Western European states.." (p. 285).

MERP: Nations that receive funding should be obligated to enter into discussion with other funded countries in order to set an agenda of participative and shared decision-making across national boundaries.

MP: Kennan wrote: "The formal initiative must come from Europeans, the program must be evolved in Europe, and without questions that the Europeans should bear the basic responsibility for it." (p. 286).

MERP: Similarly, progressive steps from the United States should only follow dialogue and planning from eligible nations. The U.S. should not initiate the Middle East, North Africa, Central Asia (MENACA) policy, but should merely provide the opportunity for serious searching and dialogue. Engagement and participation must be decided freely by invited and qualified nations.

MP: Under Secretary of State Will Clayton, one of Marshall's writers and advisors said: "If there was no aid, economic, social, and political disintegration would follow." (p. 212).

MERP: Without funding and distribution, the same pattern will follow throughout the Middle East region.

MP: Discussing the growing disintegration in Europe, Marshall argued that: it would be folly to sit back and do nothing." (p. 214).

MERP: Whether it be active violence, terrorism and biological/chemical warfare, or the calm before to a larger storm, inaction leaves much to be desired. The security of the Middle East region, and perhaps beyond, rests with those too complacent to see the results of their pettifogging and stalling.

MP: During the economic collapse in Europe between 1929 and 1931, U.S. aid to floundering Europe was insufficient and too late. The results included bank failures, bankruptcies, increased tariffs, blocked currencies, disrupted markets, and ruthless efforts at economic autocracy. These events are viewed as starting Hitler on his path. (p. 232).

MERP: Timing is critical; peace is within reach. Funds could be made appropriated; Congress can be convinced of the positive results that could emanate from a well-orchestrated and executed MERP.

MP: When President Truman launched the Marshall Plan, only 14 percent of the American people supported the idea of foreign aid. (p. 246).

MERP: Foreign assistance is now an established, almost expected form of U.S. national security policy. Certainly, the nation can be expected to question, to debate, and eventually to conclude that the United States can afford to supply the needed revenues for MERP, were other countries to withdraw financial support.

MP: The Planning Staff, according to Kennan, contributed three major elements of Marshall's speech at Harvard University: a)

Europeans should assume responsibility for initiating the program; b) the offer should be made to all Europe; and c) a decisive element should be the rehabilitation of the German economy. (p. 208).

MERP: Likewise, a) MERP policy makers should initiate the aid program; b) the offer should be made to all Arab/Muslim and regional non-Arab/Muslim nations as well as Israel; and c) primary focus should be on rehabilitating the destitute. This includes aid to Palestinians in the West Bank and Gaza, in other countries where they live in the Middle East, as well as in Afghanistan, Pakistan and other hotbeds of anti-US extremism. However, so-called moderate nations should not be taken for granted nor disregarded if Palestinians live in those places, they too should be rehabilitated.

MP: Marshall warned that: "governments, political parties or groups which seek to perpetuate human misery in order to profit therefrom politically or otherwise would encounter the opposition of the United States." (G.C.Marshall at Harvard University, June 5, 1947.) (pp. 200-201).

MERP: The same warning should apply in the Middle East, North Africa, Central Asia, and the entire area. The United States should remain firm on its commitment to human rights and social justice.

MP: "The truth of the matter is that Europe's requirements for the next three or four years of foreign food and other essential products - principally from America - were so much greater than her present ability to pay that she must have substantial additional help or face economic, social and political deterioration of a very grave character." (G.C.Marshall at Harvard University.) (p. 203).

MERP: People of the West Bank and Gaza Strip, Palestinian refugees throughout the region, and other Arab and non-Arab/Muslims living on edge remain the potential time bomb for continued chaos, violence, and terrorism. Welfare, or an equivalent term, is only a negative construct when wasted or misused. It can serve to sustain during periods of hardship; it can provide a new generation with hope and opportunity.

MP: "Our policy is directed not only against any country or doctrine but against hunger, poverty, desperation and chaos. Its purpose should be the revival of a working economy in the world so as to permit the emergence of political and social conditions in which free institutions can exist. The Soviet Union and its dependencies could participate, if they chose to." (G.C. Marshall at Harvard University.) (p. 207).

MERP: This is a doctrine worth repeating. All former enemies of Israel, Western Europe and the United States should be invited to participate.

MP: The Soviet Union's decision not to participate in the Marshall Plan, probably saved it from defeat in Congress. However, all nations involved in the European field of battle had been invited to share in the aid program. (Soviet Commissar of Foreign Affairs Molotov claimed that the Marshall Plan "would lead to nothing good.....and would split Europe into two groups of states." Furthermore, satellite countries of the Soviet Union also chose to reject participation. (p. 223).

MERP: Existing enemies of Israel, and those not friendly to the United States, including those in the Middle East, North Africa, Central Asia, Pakistan, and Afghanistan, should be approached as potential members. It is their decision whether to participate.

MP: Moscow said: "The United States was embarked with the Marshall Plan on the enslavement of Europe....all an extension of American imperialism." (p. 222).

MERP: The same call can be anticipated from numerous governments directly involved in the Palestinian/Israeli conflict, as well as from other potential MERP member governments who would argue that the United States will be "buying" its way as a means for controlling the region. Thus the increase in anti-American campaigns.

MP: Speaking before the Senate Committee, Marshall said: "This program will cost our country billions of dollars. It will impose a burden on the American taxpayer. It will require sacrifices today in order that we may enjoy security and peace tomorrow." (pp. 234-235).
MERP: This is an investment for the future; sacrifices, if any, will be few; the tradeoffs will be rewarded. The real GNP of the United States is significantly larger than it was when the Marshall Plan was offered to Europe. In the short run, the Plan and other post World War II packages cost Americans about 3 percent of their GNP for ten years. With its $10 trillion economy, the United States today is well able to afford MERP.

MP: At hearings before the House Committee on Foreign Affairs on January 12, 1948, prominent members of the panel feared passage of the Bill would result in an immediate tax hike, and worse, would be "throwing good money after bad." (p. 237).
MERP: With a bountiful economy and treasury, the United States should readily be able to support MERP. More than any other economic enterprise, MERP will stimulate the speedy recovery of the MERP nations, from the dislocations of violence, terrorism, biological/chemical attacks, and instability. The U.S. devoted a tiny of its gross domestic product to rebuild   war-torn economies in the late 1940s, or about 10 times the percentage expended on foreign aid now.

MP: Testifying before the House Committee on Foreign Affairs, Marshall said: "Durable peace requires the restoration of Western European vitality." (p. 240).
MERP: Durable peace requires the restoration of MERP and MENACA nation's vitality. President Bush has already called for

a Marshall Plan for Afghanistan and economic reform with aid for the Palestinians. Prime Minister Sharon, along with other leaders of the world, has also called for a Marshall Plan for the Palestinians. The same message will be forthcoming, directed at all other nation's of the region

MP: Congress wanted to know how soon they could expect Europe to get on its feet, and were interested in proposals for a more closely-integrated European economy. The strongest hint of a common market of Europe was established, paving the way for an eventual 15-nation European Union. (pp. 231-232).

MERP: Congress, assuredly, would seek answers to similar questions for MERP, with the expectation that a common market of MENACA would in the near future be considered. Plans for a process of institution-building and governance would be part of it.

MP: Clayton said: "The program should provide for the greatest possible European self-help, should provide for action on the part of the participating countries which they will, in fact, be able to carry out, and should be such as to assure the maintenance of the European economy without continued support from the U.S." (p. 256).

MERP: The same must apply in the MERP region. With time and hard work, self-sufficiency will likely emerge, especially following efforts at economic integration. Self-sufficiency will be written into the script for all to witness.

MP: The end of the Second World War introduced an inevitable antagonism by most Western European countries against Germany. Threats of isolation for the former enemy, wishes for division and annihilation, and permanent economic boycotts, were inevitable. The Marshall Plan dealt with most of these concerns, especially in its determination to promote future European cooperation and integration. It required an end to all talk of boycotting imports to Germany and exports from Germany.

MERP: Until 1950, Arab/Muslim and some regional non-Arab/Muslim states barred their own nations from dealing with Israel. After 1950, the Arab states banded together to blacklist shippers carrying cargo or passengers to Israel. In 1955, this list was extended to all corporations doing business with Israel. Though the boycott was cancelled, the potential threat of a future boycott against Israel remains. MERP would both serve to counter such attempts, and should include a statement in its program outlawing all forms of economic boycott against Israel and the U.S. as a condition for receiving U.S. assistance.

MP: The Administrator of the European Recovery Program found corruption and misuse of funds was greater than originally expected. New controls were put in place, further accountability was demanded, auditing of spendings was tightened, and fraudulent practices were dealt with harshly. (p. 254).

MERP: Transparency and other detailed procedures must be at the highest priority for the MERP. A tightly monitored unit must generate confidence, respect, and open disclosure, with appropriate plans for penalties and cancellations.

MP: The predecessor to the existing Organization for Economic Cooperation and Development was the Organization for European Economic Cooperation and helped coordinate post-war reconstruction under the Marshall Plan. As the first European institution dedicated to economic cooperation, the OEEC was a catalyst for economic recovery and integration on the western half of its continent. (p. 256).

MERP: Separation, disassociation, delinking, and disengagement are assuredly inappropriate, mythical concepts that will never fulfill the hope for stability, promise, nor prosperity in the region. All neighboring nations, having a common linkage, as found in the MERP region, will find a meaningful future by sharing their very best with each other.

Gordon Brown, the British Chancellor of the Exchequer argued in December 2001 that there are strong parallels between the world today and the world when the Marshall Plan of 1947 was launched. He proposed that the United States, the world's wealthiest country, should double aid to developing countries for health, education and anti-poverty efforts. This could be $50 billion annually for the next 15 years. The conditions that breed terrorism, Brown said, are similar to those that fed totalitarianism over a half-century ago. "How do you win the peace? That was the question in 1945 and it's what we face today after Afghanistan." (Brown, G., p. 41).

Chancellor Brown's challenge is no different from that in the post-World War II period. President Truman and Secretary Marshall's initial goal was to rescue Turkey and Greece from Communism but it evolved into a comprehensive plan to rebuild war-torn economies; the U.S. devoted one percent of its gross domestic product to this initiative, or about ten times the percentage expended on foreign aid in 2000. (p. 41).

It would be naïve to believe that a crisis of more than fifty years could be eliminated with a mere duplication of the 1948 Marshall Plan, first in the Middle East, then possibly in North Africa/Central Asia and beyond. Numerous, informed and well-intentioned world leaders are calling for a Marshall Plan in the Middle East region.

Nevertheless, times are quite different; forces and personalities in the world are new; attitudes and perceptions have changed; former enemies are gone replaced with others. The shift from Europe as a region possessing different history and culture, terrorism, and biological/chemical attacks expressed by non-tech groups against other technically oriented groups, all make for challenges and opportunities to create a satisfactory approach to resolving existing conflicts.

A study of the Marshall Plan is a reward in and of itself. Borrowing from all its experiences, and results, both validates the genius of its founders and administrators, and provides a basis for adding to an already-proven vehicle of cooperation, rather than merely having to invent one from scratch.

When describing how the Marshall Plan saved the free world, Secretary of State Dean Acheson, (he held the position of Secretary of State after Marshall) declared his participation in the program was being "present at the creation." (Pogue, p. 202). The European Recovery Program and the establishment of the State of Israel were declared in 1948. The two events are linked in history books--both events were dedicated to preserving freedom, both were attempting to respond to the evilness of World War II.

Fifty-five years later, Israel remains center stage, as does the Palestinian Authority, Iraq, and other nations of the Middle East, many deadlocked in a struggle for survival, power, and a rightful place in the modern world.

Jeffrey E. Garten, Dean of the Yale University School of Management presses for a worldwide economic stimulus plan, "In the immediate aftermath of World War II, the United States pushed for the establishment of the International Monetary Fund and the World Bank, and coordinated the Marshall Plan with European nations. Washington realized then that economic stability and prosperity were essential to a country's security. It's true today, too." (New York Times, The, January 11, 2003, p. A33).

In the next chapter, concepts, institutional structure, and form of governance for a proposed Middle East Recovery Program will be explained. The debates will be many and intense. They, properly so, will examine the many alternatives and options, considering inputs from the multitude of concerned parties. Motives will be suspect, passions of past and present conflicts will continue to fog the perception of humanity and stability. Patience, long a tradition of the region, will be tested. But in the end, a master plan will find both agreement and closure.

CHAPTER IV

THE MIDDLE EAST RECOVERY PROGRAM ACT

"A Palestinian state will require a vibrant economy where honest enterprise is encouraged by honest government. The United States, the international donor community and the World Bank stand ready to work with Palestinians on a major project of economic reform and development."

George W. Bush

"There isn't a more profitable undertaking for any country than to declare war on the United States and be defeated," proclaimed the fictional Grand Fenwick's prime minister in the movie *The Mouse That Roared*, "Then the Americans pour in food, machinery, clothing, technical aid and a lot of money for the relief of its former enemies."

The film was released in 1959 when the concept of nation-building to combat Communism was a significant ideology in U.S. foreign policy. Once the Soviet Union collapsed, conservatives came to nation-building as big-government waste. By the 2000 campaign, George W. Bush derided the use of American soldiers for nation-building. (*New York Times, The,* 2002, November 24). The White House is now revisiting this vital issue.

Following the September 11th attacks in New York City and Washington, DC, rebuilding other countries with aid was then considered appropriate by the Bush Administration. In November 2002 Congress passed the Afghanistan Freedom Support Act, providing $3.3 billion for reconstruction over a four year period. The legislation authorized $425 million a year for such recovery projects and set up an enterprise fund that could provide a total of $300 million in seed money to start and sustain new businesses-assuredly a mini-Marshall Plan. (*New York Times, The,* 2002, November 21).

The nation-building reversal was presented by the President of the United States in the White House Rose Garden on June 24, 2002. With George W. Bush's address, (*New York Times, The,* 2002, June 25) he opened a new period of American diplomacy in the Middle East. "The United States, the European Union, the World Bank and International Monetary Fund are willing to oversee reform in Palestinian finances, encouraging transparency and independent auditing. And the United States, along with our partners in the developed world, will increase our humanitarian assistance to relieve Palestinian suffering."

President Bush's proposed *Millennium Challenge Account* (*New York Times, The,* 2003, February 3, p. A 5) calls for the largest U.S. increase in foreign assistance in two decades. $1.3 billion would be earmarked for 2004, $2.6 billion for 2005, and $5 billion annually after that. The Plan attempts to deals with foreign aid abuses by corrupt regimes, where funds are squandered on ineffective projects and inadequate monitoring. If enacted it would offer more funding to the Middle East, but significantly alter procedures for implementation. Assuredly, it would become a major voice in the creation of MERP.

This said, funds for the Middle East Recovery Program Act would go a long way towards restoring a more civil and just society in the Middle East, but also throughout the North African and Central Asian region. Those possessing both the wisdom and authorization will have to set critical priorities that will be difficult, and assuredly will be debated. Working closely with existing regional institutions, the list of expenditures would go beyond the more traditional and obvious needs. Obvious needs are humanitarian support, infrastructure development, housing construction, employment creation, and educational-building.

By the end of 2002, U.S. Secretary of State Colin Powell introduced what he called a *Middle East Partnership Initiative* (a precursor to a Middle East Recovery Program) asking for a new effort to spread democracy and political reforms in the Middle East. He projected that the first part of the initiative contemplated adding only $29 million, which was approved by Congress in July 2002, to the $1 billion that goes for foreign aid to Arab countries. Many experts believe that the United States would spend far more than $10 billion to reconstruct the region should there be an agreement between Israel and the Palestinians. (*New York Times, The,* 2002, December 13).

And, as this volume goes to press (March 2003), the Bush administration prepared to award a contract valued at as much as $900 million (a one nation mini-Marshall Plan) to begin rebuilding a post-war Iraq, in what would be the largest government reconstruction effort since Americans helped to rebuild Germany and Japan after World War II.

Under the sponsorship of the U.S. Agency for International Development, and assuming military intervention, the awarded contractor would be required to finish the following tasks within six months:

. reopen at least half of the "economically important roads and bridges" – about 1,500 miles of roadway to high-speed traffic.

. repair 15 percent of the high-voltage electricity grid. Delivering 550 emergency generators within two months.

. provide half the population-almost 13 million people-with access to "basic health services" including at least one fully functional hospital in every major city.

. renovate several thousand schools.

. supply books and other materials to 12,500 schools.

. rehabilitate 5,000 houses and initiate "slum upgrading in major urban areas" to improve an additional 3,000 residences. (*Wall Street Journal, The,* 2003, March 10, p. A3).

FROM IRAQ TO THE WEST BANK/GAZA AND BACK

Overnight, it seems that the world is coming to grips with the reality-the devastating plight of Palestinians. In addition to the terrible loss of life in both the Palestinian Authority and Israel, according to United Nations estimates, the on-going conflict between Israelis and Palestinians has led to a doubling of Palestinian poverty and unemployment rates. "50 percent of Palestinians now live below the poverty line, and that up to 60 percent are unemployed," according to former U.S. Senator George Mitchell who testified on July 24, 2002 before the U.S. House of Representatives International Relations Committee. He said that U.N. relief officials indicate that two million Palestinians are in need of food, aid, shelter or medical assistance.

Congressman Henry Hyde, Chairman of the International Relations Committee, forcefully called for the establishment of a special temporary agency to make investments in the private sector in the Middle East aimed at sustainable job creation. He said investments by this agency should be made only if the following conditions are put into place: "...firm, measurable commitments to economic openness, including intra-regional free trade, so that growth will be continuous." (*Washington File*).

Chairman Hyde was convinced, as were other senior Congressmen, that a comprehensive economic development program for the Middle East was needed to parallel the 1948 Marshall Plan that rebuilt Western Europe following World War II. He said that the Marshall Plan in Europe dealt with the threat of renewed instability by providing reconstruction assistance and promoting economic cooperation.

Based on a study done after his trip to the Middle East, Chairman Hyde argued, "We sensed that the people who had hope of a better life in economic terms would not resort to violence. We sensed that when people had a stake in their own economic future, they should not adhere to extremist ideologies. We believed that the way towards the future was to liberalize economies, freeing them from the dead hand of outdated regulation, tariffs and other trade barriers within the region."

The ranking minority member on the International Relations Committee, Congressman Tom Lantos, a prominent thinker and continuing advocate for the Middle East peace process, offered his support for Hyde's ideas, saying that economic assistance could serve as a powerful weapon to fight terrorism. "I am extremely confident that an open, democratic Arab world is destined to prosper with the help of the American Marshall Plan you proposed." (*Washington File*).

Hyde was quick to make the point that his ideas for a Marshall Plan for the Middle East "were consistent with President Bush's recent statement that a future Palestinian state would require a vibrant economy based on honest enterprise and encouraged by honest government."

Congressman Benjamin Gilman, another senior member of the International Relations Committee believed that a Marshall Plan for the region was a "sound idea," but it must be predicated on a move toward democracy through social and economic reforms. "So too we need a Marshall Plan which focuses on religious freedom and political pluralism....We must provide those societies with the tools to repair themselves socially."

Recent findings continue to plague the social conscience of Middle East nations and the world. Only days before the House of Representatives' meeting, the United Nations Development Program (UNDP) had released its *Arab Human Development Report 2002* which highlighted a wide range of challenges that a Middle East Marshall Plan could address. "The mismatch between aspirations and their fulfillment," according to Rima Khalaf, an assistant secretary-general of the United Nations and Director of UNDP "has in some cases led to alienation and its offspring, apathy or discontent," throughout the region. "For the non-oil producing countries, this requires huge investment outlays that are currently beyond their financial means. A Marshall Plan approach can tremendously help in pulling them out of their predicament." The thrust for a Middle East Marshall Plan "can be instrumental to making that shift from a struggling region to a progressing one." (*Washington File*).

Before coming to the United Nations, Rima Khalaf served as Deputy Prime Minister of Jordan and concluded that it is possible to build "human capabilities through quality education, health and social services, and quality research and development activities, promoting creativity and technological empowerment."

The Director of UNDP, in addition, pursues using human capabilities, through utilizing the economies and providing equal opportunities to all, especially women. And on the issue of change ".... liberating human capabilities through promoting systems of good governance including the reform of state institutions and activating the voice of people."

The House of Representatives' International Relations Committee heard her call for "An equivalent of a Marshall Plan for the region cannot be timelier to provide Arab people of the region with hope and bring them closer to their aspirations for a better life. (*Washington File*).

"As a soldier who knows the horrors of war," spoke Prime Minister Ariel Sharon in April 2002, "I seek a peace with every Arab country. We are ready to share our know-how with Palestinians, to help you and be helped by you. I see a Marshall Plan for Palestine - call it the Bush-Sharon plan - to solve your problem of unemployment. Together we can make tremendous achievements." (Safire).

The MERP process will most likely begin in the disputed areas of the Middle East, (in theory, it could start in North Africa and/or Central Asia). For disputed areas, consideration should be given to utilizing significant monies for relocating Israelis from West Bank/Gaza settlements, for renovating their abandoned facilities to be used by returning Palestinian refugees, for assisting in the return of Palestinians to either Israel or to the newly-established Palestinian state, for compensating Israelis for lands and property confiscated because of leaving their original homelands, and for other legitimate purposes.

MERP could readily commence as MENARP - Middle East/North Africa Recovery Program, or indeed as MENACARP - Middle East/North Africa/Central Asia Recovery Program. Some would argue that the latter would be ideal, but pragmatic needs of the day, including financial and political needs, might require consideration of additions for a later time. However, events since 9/11/01 may necessitate changing all approaches.

The recovery effort should commence with assistance to the Palestinians, then to other Middle East nations. To anticipate the probability that a match can be found along the way, it is desirable to anticipate nations of North Africa and Central Asia entering the recovery program. Consequently, all geographically-eligible countries, including past or present enemies, should be invited at the outset to participate in dialogue with Middle East states to offer statements of need, and then, to await the time when they will be factored into the providing of assistance.

A MISGUIDED APPROACH IN AFGHANISTAN

Unfortunately, the nation-rebuilding program in Afghanistan, more than one year after the response to 9/11, had not pursued an effective format. This approach assuredly should not become a working model for aid in the Middle East. While the military, primarily U.S., developed important road and bridge projects and helped rebuild scores of schools, irrigation systems and health clinics in nearly one dozen provinces, this approach was ill-timed, was ineffective for the long term, and may fail to accomplish its intended goals.

Afghan officials and donors estimated that the government would need at least $10 billion to rebuild its shattered economy. The World Bank representative identified six priority areas for development: education, roads, water and power, rebuilding of government buildings nationwide, water and sanitation in the cities and rural development.

(The United Nation's Development Program expected that the effort in Afghanistan would cost up to $6.5 billion for the first 30 months, and should there be a regime-change in Iraq resulting from intrusion into her politics, rebuilding Iraq would cost $30 B.) (*New York Times, The,* 2003, January 31, p. A10.)

Many critics say that the Pentagon's new plans fall well short of a pledge by President Bush to work "in the best traditions of George Marshall." Rather than getting out there in a leadership role and saying "We need a Marshall Plan, and fighting for it, they've taken a minimalist approach," said Joel Charny, Vice President for Policy with Refugees International. (*New York Times, The,* November 12, 2002).

The Palestinians have received more aid per-capita than those aided by the 1948 Marshall Plan. The aid has increased since the beginning of the violence. The following table summarizes the aid assessment: *The Marshall Plan vs. Palestinian Assistance.* (AIPAC, September 9, 2002).

Aid Recipients	Duration of Aid	Total Amount of Aid	Amount per Person	Amount Person/ Year
EUROPEANS	4 years	$60 billion*	$272	$68
PALESTINIANS	9 years	$4 billion	$1,330	$161

* reflects equivalent in today's dollars

On December 15, 2001, an Italian-sponsored "Extraordinary Initiative for the Reconstruction and Development of the Palestinian Economy" was approved by the Council of Ministers of the European Union at its Laeken European Council meeting. Underlying this major idea was the hope that the prospect of a future of shared prosperity might spur the parties engaged in the conflict to take a decisive step forward and embark upon the final negotiations for the constitution of a Palestinian state. (Antonio Badini, *LIMES*, Rivista Italiana di Geopolitica).

The EU time frame was 10 years, with the first five being the most critical. Giving a new impetus to the dialogue on regional cooperation, the total funding required for the initiative was estimated to be around 6.2 billion euros ($6.2 billion) for the first five years as follows:

Millions of euros

Production......................................	1,510
Infrastructure...................................	2,750
Social and Humanitarian sector..............	1,140
Training, technical assistance and scientific cooperation....................................	800

Furthermore, Elmer L. Winter, Chairman of the *Committee for Economic Growth of Israel* proposed in the summer 2002 a Middle East Economic Development (MEED) Plan through the economic development of the area - based on the creation of 320,000 jobs for Palestinians and 100,000 for the Israelis. (Winter, Elmer L., July 2002).

MOVING FORWARD

Inclusion of all MENACA nations at the outset would demand (a) a signed statement from each entity that it will recognize the rights of all members to exist (including the State of Israel and the Palestinian state.), (b) cancellation of all acts of aggression against another member nation, including terrorist acts, boycotts, etc., to qualify as a potential recipient of U.S. assistance, and (c) renunciation of violence and terrorism, economic boycotts, and other acts detrimental to the economic and political stability of the region.

The bills presented to the House of Representatives and to the Senate should be all-inclusive of the 28 nations that might become partners, and should call the legislation, the Middle East/North Africa/Central Asia Recovery Program. Alternatively, should the mood of the moment only wish to consider a Middle

East Recovery Program, so it shall be. However, the record should indicate that a more appropriate, expansive effort should also include the nations of North Africa, plus those of Central Asia, Pakistan, Afghanistan, and Turkey.

With extensive borrowing, assessing, and evaluating from Public Law 472, from the Legislative history of the Foreign Assistance Act that went before the House, (Report No. 185-March 20, 1948) and from the Act that went before the Senate, (Report No. 935-February 26, 1948), guidelines are given in the following pages for the Middle East Recovery Program (MERP) legislation. This descriptive outline identifies concepts of institution-building and governance which will be open to debate, alteration, and change.   Crystal ball gazing encourages this exchange.

The intent below is to identify principal issues and approaches that have proven successful in earlier legislation, and from which can be learned significant lessons from history.

Equally appropriate to the PROPOSED Middle East Recovery Program is the introduction of the Foreign Assistance Act of 1948, which stated: "An Act to promote world peace and the general welfare, national interest, and foreign policy of the United States through economic, financial, and other measures necessary to the maintenance of conditions abroad in which free institutions may survive and consistent with the maintenance of the strength and stability of the United States." (Foreign Assistance Act of 1948).

A. DOLLAR REQUIREMENTS OF THE RECOVERY PROGRAM

Estimates of the volume and kinds of commodities that will, in fact, be required to enable the countries of the Middle East/North Africa/Central Asia to effect economic reconstruction are necessarily subject to wide margins of error. The wide margins are due to the variety of assumptions upon which the estimates are made, including possible changes in prices, commodities, and availability of supplies.

B. REGIONAL FOCUS, NOT NATIONAL

At the very heart of the philosophy of the recovery program lies the hope that the Middle East/North Africa/Central Asia will develop on a regional basis rather than along the lines of national self-sufficiencies. Hopefully, the countries will volunteer actions that make them economically inter-dependent as opposed to economically self-sufficient.

For an objective of voluntary regional development, there clearly can be no pre-arranged pattern. To have one, and to establish the controls and means of enforcement that would be necessary to bring it into being, would necessitate the use of some of the very kinds of outside pressures to which the United States and other democratic nations are unalterably opposed.

C. WORK OF A PLANNING CONFERENCE

Prior to presenting a bill for enactment to the Congress, all interested and invited parties (hopefully at the foreign ministry level) of the MENA region (perhaps expanded to include MENACA nations) should be brought together to work out a joint program for their own recovery. They then would have to match the commodity and equipment requirements of such a program against their own resources so as to arrive at estimates of needs from non-MENACA sources.

It might be expected that the figures their experts work up can in many cases be questioned, or that they may not leave much to be desired in allowing for regional, as opposed to nationalistic development. But rather, the remarkable fact might be that they are able to agree upon anything at all definitive.

The conference should attempt to arrive at estimates of need as a function of each country's net balance-of-payments position with the United States and to arrive at a total figure for combined countries. It can be expected that this group will add up the individual country estimates of requirements and present the totals as to the need for the entire area. This procedure, however could result in overstated national requirements where national economic ambition is inflated instead of relating to members of a closely-coordinated economic group.

D. SCREENING BY UNITED STATES EXPERTS

U.S. experts, formed into committees, will review the received information and data. The conclusions of these committees should serve as the administration's report to be submitted by the Department of State to Congress, together with the administration's proposed draft legislation. Fine tuning will be needed at all times.

E. BASIC OBLIGATIONS OF PARTICIPATION

First, the nations within the scope of this program will qualify for assistance through the steps, of joining with other nations concerned interested in restoration of the Middle East, North Africa and Central Asia economy. Second, the nations will sign bilateral agreements with the United States.

In order to ensure that the recovery program is carried out, the participating countries will pledge themselves to join together, and invite other MENACA (also Pakistan, Afghanistan and Turkey) countries to join with them, in working towards regional economic integration. This pledge will be undertaken by each country with respect to its own national program, but it will also take into account similar pledges made by the other participating countries. In particular, each country will undertake to use all its efforts:

(a) to develop its production to reach set targets;
(b) to make the fullest and most effective use of its existing productive capacity including all available manpower;
(c) to modernize its equipment and transportation, so that labor becomes more productive, conditions of work are improved, and standards of living of all MENACA citizens are raised;

(d) to apply all necessary measures leading to the rapid achievement of internal financial monetary and economic stability while maintaining in each country a high level of employment;

(e) to cooperate with one another and with like-minded countries in all possible steps to reduce tariffs and other barriers to the expansion of trade between themselves and the rest of the world, in accordance with the rules and regulations of the World Trade Organization;

(f) to progressively remove the obstacles to the free movement of persons within the MENACA region;

(g) to organize and utilize the means by which common resources can be developed in partnership;

(h) to assist in the resettling of Palestinian refugees, and Israeli settlers now in the West Bank and Gaza Strip;

(i) to refrain from any form of physical aggression, including terrorism and/or biological/chemical attacks against any other nation that applies for and is accepted to receive funding from MERP;

(j) to move in the direction of a more open, civil, free, accountable, and transparent society; and

(k) to desist from any form of economic boycott against other MENACA nations.

Required pledges in the bilateral agreements should include the undertaking of steps necessary to eliminate abnormal outside aid.

Pledges in regard to money and finance should be in the direction of movement toward stable currency, proper exchange rates, and restored confidence in national currencies.

International trade pledges should require cooperation to increase the interchange of goods and services and to reduce trade barriers.

It is hoped that all nations of MENACA will both participate and receive U.S. assistance. Basically, they would qualify for aid if they are in need, and if they support cooperation and stability with all other recipients. Because it is urgent to move MERP forward with speed, it is conceivable that some countries, for a host of reasons, will either choose not to apply outright, or will find that they cannot qualify for immediate participation.

Provisions should be made to extend the process of joining MENACA and late-comers can ascend, without prejudice. However, all MENACA nations, no matter what barriers may exist for entry, both short- and long-term, should join with others at the planning conference to identify their financial ability with or without MERP support. Their initial participation would, importantly, also show that they were involved from the outset of the Act's passage.

In the next section, regular print identifies a proposed entry for the Act, while Italic print identifies dialogue and analysis to explain rationale for the entry.

Section 1. THE MIDDLE EAST RECOVERY PROGRAM ACT

This TITLE may be cited as the Middle East Recovery Program, or more specifically, the Middle East (ME) Economic Cooperation Act.

Prior to the passage and implementation of the Marshall Plan, eligible nations of Western Europe met with a newly-formed Committee of European Economic Cooperation at Paris in September 1947. Members signed a report of the Committee, thus qualifying for participation in the Plan and for receiving assistance.

The Middle East Recovery Program (MERP) Act will emphasize two fundamental aspects: (1) that the assistance is economic in character; and (2) that the success of MERP requires cooperation among the countries participating in the program.

To clarify "countries participating in the program"-initially MERP is envisioned to include nations contiguous to Israel. But, other Arab/Muslim and non-Arab/Muslim countries, also part of the Middle East (referred to by the U.S. State

Department as the Near East) will be eligible. Likewise, all other Arab nations, extending as far west as Morocco, will also be candidates.

Therefore, long-term MERP can be extended to be called MENACARP, Middle East/North Africa/Central Asia Recovery Program. When applicable MENACA will be a more than adequate substitute for ME.

Section 2. FINDINGS AND DECLARATION OF POLICY
(a)

Recognizing the intimate economic and other relationships between the United States and the nations of the Middle East/North Africa/Central Africa (MENACA), and recognizing that disruption following in the wake of violence and terrorism is not contained by national frontiers, the Congress finds that the existing situation in the region endangers the establishment of a lasting peace, the general welfare and national interest of the United States, and the attainment of the objectives of the United Nations.

The restoration or maintenance in MENACA nations of principles of individual liberty, free institutions, and genuine independence rests largely upon the establishment of sound economic conditions, stable international economic relationships, and the achievement by the countries of MENACA region of a healthy economy independent of extraordinary outside assistance.

The accomplishment of these objectives calls for a plan of MENACA recovery, that is open to all such nations that cooperate in such a plan, that is based upon a strong production effort, that expands foreign trade, that creates and maintains internal financial stability, and that develops economic cooperation, including implementing steps to establish and maintain equitable rates of exchange and bringing about the progressive elimination of trade barriers.

Mindful of the advantages that the United States, the European Union and some other trading blocs have enjoyed through the existence of large regional markets with no internal trade barriers, and believing that similar advantages can accrue to the countries of MENACA, it is declared to be the policy of the people of the United States to encourage these countries through a joint organization to exert sustained common effort as set forth in the report of the Committee of Middle East/North Africa/Central Asia Economic Cooperation, which intends to achieve economic cooperation in MENACA, and which is essential for lasting peace and prosperity.

It is further declared to be the policy of the people of the United States to sustain and strengthen principles of individual liberty, free institutions, and genuine independence of MENACA, which would participate in a joint recovery program based upon self-help and mutual cooperation.

It is further declared to be the policy of the people of the United States to assist in the creation of a Palestinian state where Palestinians may live if they choose and/or compensate Palestinians for their decades of separation, also to utilize funds for the exodus of Israeli settlers out of the West Bank and/or Gaza Strip. Additionally, there will be discussions and possible actions to compensate Jews who left their Arab homelands to resettle within the state of Israel. (The increasing plight of Central Asia refugees must be reexamined as a separate effort of the United Nations and not be muddled with the above.)

Assuredly, the general welfare and national interests of the United States are intimately related to the existence of a healthy MENACA. The great objectives of a MERP cannot be achieved solely by economic measures, and, therefore, political conditions are to be included as a shaper of events.

In addition, there must be a willingness and ability of the peoples of the participating states to recognize and emphasize their areas of common interest, rather than their points of difference and separation, and to concentrate their efforts upon devising means for closer cooperation.

Reference to a "plan for Middle East recovery" is designed to make clear that the recovery program undertaken by nations of MENACA must be a developing, not a static, program.

To aid Middle East refugees in their resettlement, whether Arab/Muslim, or non-Arab Muslim, or Jew, is a worthy expenditure of the recovery program. Without this resolution, little progress on other critical issues for development, restoration, and cooperation will be halted. Likewise, consideration can be given to use some assistance funds to compensate Jewish citizens of Arab descent who were forced to flee their homeland following 1948 and until the end of 1967.

(b)
PURPOSES OF A RECOVERY PROGRAM
The purpose of the recovery program is to aid participating countries by furnishing material and financial assistance. Through their own individual and concerted efforts, the countries will hopefully become independent of extraordinary outside economic assistance within the period of operations, by:

(1) promoting industrial and agricultural production in the participating countries;

(2) furthering the restoration or maintenance of the soundness of MENACA currencies, budgets, and finances;

(3) facilitating and stimulating the growth of international trade of participating countries with one another and with other countries by appropriate measures including reduction of barriers which may hamper such trade.

Economic cooperation among the participating countries is dependent upon the political realities in those countries. It is therefore critical that the objectives of the recovery program be stated in a manner sufficiently broad to enable the Administrator, when determining the form and measure of assistance to be given to a participating country, to take into consideration the varied factors which will bear upon the success of this undertaking.

Section 3. PARTICIPATING COUNTRIES
    To include any MENACA entity whose ranking representative signed the report of the Committee of Middle East/North Africa/Central Asia Economic Cooperation.
    Participating countries are eligible if they become a participant in a joint effort for Middle East/North Africa/Central Asia recovery and only for so long as each government remains an adherent to such a program. Certain of the participating nations who do not require assistance will, nevertheless, join in the program for the purpose of cooperating with the other countries in carrying out the mutual effort which is inherent in the recovery plan.

Section 4. ESTABLISHMENT OF MIDDLE EAST/NORTH AFRICA/ CENTRAL ASIA ECONOMIC COOPERATION ADMINISTRATION
(a)
    There is hereby established, with its principal office in the District of Columbia, an agency of the Government which shall be known as the Middle East/North Africa/Central Asia Economic Cooperation Administration, hereinafter referred to as the Administration. The Administration shall be headed by an Administrator for MENACA Economic Cooperation, hereinafter referred to as the Administrator, who shall be appointed by the U.S. President, by and with the advice and consent of the Senate.
    The Administrator shall be responsible to the President of the United States and shall have a status in the executive branch of the Government comparable to that of the head of an executive department. Except, as otherwise provided in this title, the administration of the provisions of this title is hereby vested in the Administrator and his functions shall be performed under the control of the President.
    The Administrator will have a status which will put him or her on a footing of equality with the heads of other agencies and departments of the Government, and he or she will have the

right of direct access to the President, under whose leadership functions will be performed.

(b)

The Deputy Administrator for MENACA Economic Cooperation shall perform such functions as the Administrator shall designate, and shall be Acting Administrator for MENACA Economic Cooperation during the absence or disability of the Administrator or in the event of a vacancy in the office of Administrator.

The Deputy Administrator is authorized to perform any functions delegated to him or her by the Administrator, or, in the event of a vacancy in the office of the Administrator, he or she will be Acting Administrator.

(c)

The President is authorized, pending the appointment and qualification of the first Administrator or Deputy Administrator for MENACA Economic Cooperation appointed hereunder, to provide, for a period of not to exceed thirty days after the date of enactment of this Act, for the performance of the functions of the Administrator under this recovery program through such departments, agencies, or establishments of the United States Government as he or she may direct. In the event the President nominates an Administrator or Deputy Administrator after the expiration of such thirty-day period, the authority conferred upon the President by this subsection shall be extended beyond such thirty-day period but only until an Administrator or Deputy Administrator qualifies and takes office.

The intent is to assure commencement of operations as soon as possible following passage, even if it may not have been possible for the first Administrator or his Deputy to take office.

Section 5. GENERAL FUNCTIONS OF THE ADMINIS-TRATOR

(a)

The Administrator, under the control of the President, shall, in addition to all other functions vested in him or her by this recovery program,

(1) review and appraise the requirements of participating countries for assistance under the terms of this program;

(2) formulate programs using United States assistance under this program, and approve specific projects which have been submitted to him or her by the participating countries;

(3) provide for the efficient execution of any such programs as may be placed in operation; and

(4) terminate provision of assistance or take other remedial action as provided.

The authority of the Administrator to formulate programs of United States assistance includes authority to approve specific projects which may be proposed to him or her by a participating country, to be undertaken by such country in substantial part with assistance furnished under the recovery program.

The authority reposed in the Administrator to provide for the efficient execution of programs refers to the effective performance on the part of agencies of the U.S. Government with respect to services rendered by such agencies. Services for approved programs could include procurement, storage, and transportation.

The authority to terminate provision of assistance or take other remedial action relates to the responsibility of the Administrator to take appropriate action to assure that assistance under this recovery program is provided only in accordance with its provisions and its stated purposes. Inasmuch as the termination of the provision of assistance undoubtedly would have serious implications with respect to the foreign-policy objectives of the U.S., it is not contemplated that such action would be taken without consultation with the Secretary of State. Moreover, in some circumstances, certain action by the Administrator, or by other agencies of the Government, might be more appropriate than termination of the provision of assistance. Accordingly, the Administrator may provide for, or recommend to the President or to the appropriate agency of the Government, the taking of such other action

(b)

In order to strengthen and make more effective the conduct of the foreign relations of the United States -

(1) the Administrator and the Secretary of State shall keep each other fully and currently informed on matters, including perspective action, arising within the scope of their respective duties which are pertinent to the duties of the other;

(2) when the Secretary of State believes that any action, proposed action, or failure to act on the part of the Administrator is inconsistent with the foreign-policy objectives of the United States, he or she shall consult with the Administrator and, if differences of view are not adjusted by consultation, the matter shall be referred to the President for final decision;

(3) whenever the Administrator believes that any action, proposed action, or failure to act on the part of the Secretary of State in performing functions under this title is inconsistent with the purposes and provisions of this title, he shall consult with the Secretary of State and, if differences of view are not adjusted by consultation, the matter shall be referred to the President for final decision.

To strengthen and make more effective the conduct of foreign relations of the U.S., the Administrator and the U.S. Secretary of State will work closely together. Should there arise matters of conflict between the two of them, the President shall serve as final arbiter.

Section 6. NATIONAL ADVISORY COUNCIL

In order to coordinate the policies and operations of the representatives of the U.S. and of all agencies of the government which make or participate in making foreign loans or which engage in foreign financial, exchange or monetary transactions, there is hereby established the National Advisory council (hereinafter referred to as the Council), consisting of the Secretary of the Treasury, Chair, the U.S. Secretary of State, the Secretary of Commerce, the Secretary of Homeland Security, the Chair of the Board of Governors of the Federal Reserve System, the Chair of the Board of Directors of the Export-Import Bank of Washington, the head of the Trade Representatives Office, and during such period as the MENACA Economic Cooperation Administration shall continue to exist, the Administrator for MENACA Economic Cooperation.

In view of the important aspects of foreign financial exchange and monetary transactions which will be involved in the development of policies under this title, the Administrator is made a member of the National Advisory Council during the existence of the Administration.

Section 7. PUBLIC ADVISORY BOARD
(a)

A Public Advisory Board, hereinafter referred to as the Board, shall advise and consult with the Administrator with respect to general or basic policy matters arising in connection with the Administrator's discharge of his or her responsibilities. The Board shall consist of the Administrator, who shall be Chair, and shall not exceed twelve additional members to be appointed by the President, by and with the advice and consent of the Senate, and who shall be selected from among citizens of the United States of broad and varied experience in matters affecting the public interest. Officers and employees of the United States who, as such, regularly receive compensation for current services shall be ineligible to serve on the Board.

The Board shall meet at least once a month and at other times upon the call of the Administrator or when three or more members of the Board request the Administrator to call a meeting. Not more than a majority of two of the members shall be appointed to the Board from the same political party.

A Public Advisory Board is needed to advise and consult with the Administrator with respect to general or basic policy matters. The creation of such a board is desirable both from the standpoint of making available to the Administrator the benefit of the advice and experience of private citizens representing broad public interests and also from the standpoint of assuring the fullest practicable degree of public information concerning the programs and operations under this recovery plan.   Board members shall represent business, labor, agriculture, the professions and other areas affecting the public interest.

Members of the Board are to be appointed by the President, with the consent of the Senate.

(b)

The Administrator may appoint such other advisory committees as he or she may determine to be necessary or desirable to effectuate the purposes of this recovery program.

As required by the Administrator, experts and consultants shall be employed by the Administrator.

Section 8. UNITED STATES SPECIAL REPRESENTATIVE ABROAD

There shall be a U.S. Special Representative in the Middle East/North Africa/Central Asia region who shall (a) be appointed by the President, by and with the advice and consent of the Senate, (b) be entitled to receive the same compensation and allowances as a chief of mission, and (c) have the rank of ambassador extraordinary and plenipotentiary.

He or she shall be the representative of the Administrator, and shall also be the chief representative of the United States Government to any organization of participating countries which may be established by such countries to further a joint program for recovery, and shall discharge, on site, such additional responsibilities as may be assigned by the Administrator, with the approval of the President in furtherance of the purposes of this recovery program. He or she shall receive instructions from the

Administrator, and such instructions shall be prepared and transmitted to him or her in accordance with procedures agreed to between the Administrator and the Secretary of State in order to assure appropriate coordination.

He or she shall inform the Administrator, the Secretary of State, the chiefs of the U.S. diplomatic missions, and the chiefs of the special missions abreast of his or her activities.

He or she shall consult with the chiefs of all such missions, who shall give him such cooperation as he or she may require for the performance of duties under this title.

The U.S. representative in the Middle East/North Africa/Central Asia region will play a key role in the accomplishment of the purposes of this recovery program, serving as the chief representative of the U.S. Government to the continuing organization set up by the participating countries.

He or she will receive instructions from the Administrator, which shall be prepared and transmitted in such a manner as to assure the necessary effective coordination between the Administrator and the Secretary of State.

Activities of the Representative should also be shared with the Senate Foreign Relations Committee Chair, the House Foreign Affairs Committee, the Senate Appropriations Committee, and the House Appropriations Committee.

Section 9. SPECIAL MIDDLE EAST/NORTH AFRICA/CENTRAL ASIA ECONOMIC COOPERATION MISSIONS ABROAD
(a)
There shall be established for each participating country, a special mission for economic cooperation under the direction of a director who shall be responsible for assuring the performance within such country of operations. The directors shall be appointed by the Administrator, shall receive instructions from the Administrator, and shall report to the Administrator on the performance of duties assigned.

In order to assure the proper performance within each of the participating countries of operations, a special mission for economic cooperation within each such country under the direction of a director who is to be appointed by the Administrator shall exist. The special mission representative shall receive instructions from the Administrator, and shall report to him or her on the performance of assigned duties.

(b)

The director of the special mission shall keep the chief of the U.S. diplomatic mission fully and currently informed on matters, including prospective actions, arising within the scope of the operations of the special mission. Additionally, the director of the diplomatic mission shall keep the director of the special mission fully and currently informed on matters relative to the conduct of the duties of the director of the special mission.

The director of the U.S. diplomatic mission will be responsible for assuring that the operations of the special mission are consistent with the foreign-policy objectives of the United States in such country and to that end whenever the director of the U.S. diplomatic mission believes that any action, proposed action, or failure to act on the part of the special mission is inconsistent with such foreign-policy objectives, he or she shall so advise the director of the special mission and the U.S. Special Representative in the region.

If differences of view are not adjusted by consultation, the matter shall be referred to the Secretary of State and the Administrator for decisions.

This subsection deals with proper coordination between the director of the special mission and the director of the U.S. diplomatic mission. In the event of disagreement between the Secretary of State and the Administrator, the matter would be referred to the President for final decision.

Section 10. PERSONNEL OUTSIDE THE UNITED STATES

No citizen or resident of the United States may be employed, or if already employed, may be assigned to duties by the Secretary of State or the Administrator under this recovery program for a period to exceed three months unless such individual has been investigated as to loyalty and security by the Federal Bureau of Investigation, and a report has been made to the Secretary of State and the Administrator, and until the Secretary of State or the Administrator has certified in writing (and filed copies thereof with the Senate Committee on Foreign Relations and the House Committee on Foreign Affairs) that, after full consideration of such report, he believes such individual is loyal to the United States, its Constitution, and form of government, and is not now and has never been a member of any organization advocating contrary views. This subsection shall not apply in the case of any officer appointed by the President by and with the advice and consent of the Senate.

In the sensitive area of the Middle East/North Africa/Central Asia, careful screening of candidates is needed both to provide security and allegiance to the United States and to provide participating nations with a confidence that involved representatives of the United States are "honest brokers" who seek a fair and equitable solution to the myriad of problems. The Federal Bureau of Investigation, by its design and history, is the appropriate venue for background checks on U.S. participants in the Program.

Individuals chosen directly by the President of the United States, may be verified by the Federal Bureau of Investigation, but verification can be bypassed at the President's choice, as long as there is "advice and consent of the Senate."

Section 11. NATURE AND METHOD OF ASSISTANCE
(a)

The Administrator may, from time to time, furnish assistance to any participating country when he or she deems it to be in furtherance of the purposes of this title, to be included in the terms and conditions set forth in this recovery program, to be consistent with the provisions of this plan, and to be necessary and proper.

(1) Procuring from any source, including Government stocks, which the Administrator determines to be required for the furtherance of the purposes of this recovery program.

(2) Processing, storing, transporting, and repairing any goods or performing any other services with respect to a participating country which the Administrator determines to be required for accomplishing the purposes of this recovery program.

(3) Procuring and furnishing technical information and assistance.

(4) Transferring of any commodity or service, which transfer shall be signified by delivery of the custody and right of possession and use of each commodity, or otherwise making available any such commodity, or rendering a service to a participating country or to any agency or organization representing a participating country.

(5) Allocating of goods or services to specific projects designed to carry out the purposes of this recovery program, which have been submitted to the Administrator by participating countries and have been approved by him or her.

This section prescribes the forms and procedures by which the Administrator may provide assistance to a participating country, and the methods of furnishing such assistance.

The Administrator can provide assistance to any participating country. He may provide for procurement of any commodity which he or she determines to be required for the furtherance of the purposes of the recovery program.

It will permit the procurement of goods outside of the U.S. that are in short supply in the U.S., thereby relieving shortages in this country, and it will also reduce the inflationary effect of increased demands for certain commodities from U.S. sources.

(b)

In order to facilitate and maximize the use of private channels of trade, subject to adequate safeguards to assure that all expenditures in connection with such procurement are within approved programs in accordance with terms and conditions established by the Administrator, he or she may provide for the performance of any of the functions described in subsection (a) of this section,

(1) by establishing accounts against which, under regulations prescribed by the Administrator which include:

(A) letters of commitment constituting obligations of the U.S.

(B) withdrawals made by participating countries, or agencies or organizations representing participating countries or by other persons or organizations, upon presentation of contracts, invoices, or other documentation specified by the Administrator to assure the use of such withdrawals for purposes approved by the Administrator.

(2) by utilizing the services and facilities of any department, agency, or establishment of Government as the President shall direct, or with the consent of the head of such department, agency, or establishment.

(3) by making, under rules and regulations to be prescribed by the Administrator, guarantees to any person of investment in connection with projects approved by the Administrator and the participating country concerned as furthering the purposes of this recovery program.

This subsection prescribes the method under which the Administrator may provide the types of assistance authorized.

Section 12. PROTECTION OF DOMESTIC ECONOMY

The Administrator shall provide for the procurement in the U.S. of commodities under this recovery program in such a way as to (1) minimize the drain upon the resources of the United States and the impact of such procurement upon the domestic economy, and (2) avoid impairing the fulfillment of vital needs of the people of the United States.

This provision is designed to assure the protection of the domestic economy.

Section 13. BILATERAL AND MULTILATERAL UNDERTAKINGS
(a)

The Secretary of State, after consultation with the Administrator, is authorized to conclude, with individual participating countries or any number of such countries or with an organization representing any such countries, agreements in furtherance of the purposes of this recovery program.

The Secretary of State, before an Administrator or Deputy Administrator shall have qualified and taken office, is authorized to negotiate and conclude such temporary agreements in implementation of subsection (b) of this section as he may deem necessary in furtherance of the purposes of this recovery program. When an Administrator or Deputy Administrator shall have qualified and taken office, the Secretary of State shall conclude the basic agreements required by subsection (b) of this section only after consultation with the Administrator or Deputy Administrator, as the case may be.

This section is designed to assure that (a) in accordance with the declaration of policy, continuity of assistance provided under this recovery program will be dependent upon continuity of cooperation among countries participating in the program, and (b) as a condition precedent to receiving such assistance, each participating country shall make an executive agreement with the United States embodying undertakings essential to the accomplishment of the purposes of this recovery program.
(b)

The provision of assistance under this recovery program results from the multilateral pledges of the participating countries to use all their efforts to accomplish a joint recovery program based upon self-help and mutual cooperation. Assistance is contingent upon continuous effort of the participating countries to accomplish a joint recovery program through multilateral undertakings and to establish a continuing organization for this purpose. In addition to continued mutual cooperation of the participating countries in such a program, each such country shall conclude an agreement with the United States Government in order for such a country to be eligible to receive assistance under this recovery program. Such agreement shall provide for the adherence of each country to the purposes of this title and shall, where applicable, make appropriate provision, among others, for:

(1) promoting industrial and agricultural production in order to enable the participating country to become independent of extraordinary outside economic assistance;

(2) taking financial and monetary measures necessary to stabilize its currency, establishing or maintaining a valid rate of exchange, balancing its governmental budget as soon as practicable, and generally to restoring or maintaining confidence in its monetary system.

(3) facilitating and stimulating increased interchange of goods and services among the participating countries as well as between MENACA and with other countries and reducing barriers to trade among themselves as well as with other countries;

(4) making efficient and practical use, within the framework of a joint program for recovery, of the resources of such participating country;

(5) publishing in such country and transmitting to the U.S., not less frequently than every calendar quarter after the date of the agreement, full statements of operations under the agreement, including a report of the use of funds, commodities, and services received under this recovery program;

(6) furnishing promptly, upon request of the U.S., any relevant information which would be of assistance to the United States in determining the nature and scope of operations and the use of assistance under this recovery program.

To encourage continued cooperation, which envisages multilateral reciprocal pledges given by the participating countries among themselves, to use all their efforts to accomplish a joint recovery program based upon self-help and mutual cooperation, and including the establishment of a continuing organization for that purpose, is required.

In addition to the multilateral reciprocal pledges to be given among themselves, each participating country will be required to conclude an executive agreement with the U.S. providing for the adherence of such country to the purposes of this recovery program.

Section 14. INVOLVEMENT FROM AROUND THE WORLD

The President shall take appropriate steps to encourage all countries throughout the world to make available to participating entities such assistance as they may be able to furnish.

The United States, hopefully, should not alone provide total aid to participating countries. When feasible, other nations, specifically from the European Union, Japan, and Russia, plus others that are able, should be willing to contribute.

Section 15. TERMINATION OF ASSISTANCE

The Administrator, in determining the form and measure of assistance provided under this recovery program to any participating country, shall take into account the extent to which such country is complying with its pledges to other participating countries and with its agreement concluded with the United States.

The Administrator shall terminate the provision of assistance under this recovery program to any participating country whenever he or she determines that (1) such country is not adhering to its agreement, or is diverting from the purposes of this recovery program. In circumstances, remedial action other than termination will not more effectively promote the purposes of this recovery program, or (2) because of changed conditions such as assistance no longer consistent with the national interest of the U.S. Termination of assistance to any country shall include the termination of deliveries of all supplies scheduled under the aid program for such country and not yet delivered.

This section is to assure that continuity of assistance under the program will be conditional upon compliance with undertakings by the participating country receiving assistance. In certain cases, the Administrator may determine that some corrective or preventive action may be more appropriate than termination of assistance. Termination of assistance would, to the extent possible, include termination of scheduled deliveries.

Section 16.   UNITED NATIONS AND THE EUROPEAN UNION

The President is authorized to request the cooperation of or the use of the services and facilities of the United Nations, its organs and specialized agencies, or other international organizations, in particular the European Union, in carrying out the purposes of this recovery program, and may make payments, by advancements or reimbursements, for such purposes, out of funds made available for the purposes of this recovery program.

As deemed necessary, the President shall cause to be transmitted to the Secretary General of the United Nations and to the President of the Commission of the European Union, copies of reports to Congress on the operations conducted under this recovery program.

Any agreements concluded between the U.S. and participating countries, or groups of such countries, in implementation of the purposes of this recovery program, shall be registered with the United Nations if such registration is required by the Charter of the United Nations. Such agreements shall also be registered with the Council of Ministers, Parliament, and Commission of the European Union, and any other governmental bodies as needed.

The United Nations, the European Union and others, such as Russia, Japan, etc., are to receive reports and listings of MERP actions. All agreements resulting from this program shall also be presented to the United Nations and to the European Union, and other governments as deemed appropriate.

Section 17. REPORTS TO CONGRESS

The President from time to time, but not less frequently than once every calendar quarter, and once every year until all operations under this recovery program have been completed, shall transmit to the Congress a report of operations under this recovery program, including the bilateral and multilateral agreements entered into as a result of carrying out the provisions of MERP.

*   *   *   *   *   *   *   *   *   *   *   *   *   *   *   *

Between the end of World War II in 1945 and 1947, the United States had already loaned or given nearly $6 billion (today equal to more than $60 billion) to save the starving and unemployed in Europe, both friend and foe. Working with existing regional organizations, the Marshall Plan was the natural next step. The restoration of Western Europe's economy with the eventual evolution of the European Economic Community clearly vilified the U.S. role in its foreign-aid developmental effort.

Transparency, accountability and corruption remain critical issues in the Middle East. The existing short-sighted amount of promised funding will only lead to greater friction in the near future. Let's learn from the Marshall Plan and with pride, open our wallets to permit a more meaningful outpouring of funds that can parallel the great accomplishments of the recovery program following the end of World War II. MERP can now move the process to a higher level and emulate the wonders and successes resulting from the 1948 Marshall Plan.

CHAPTER V

THE PATH TOWARDS ECONOMIC INTEGRATION

*"The effort to increase regional economic cooperation is not -
as some seem to feel - a favor to any particular nation. Shared
prosperity will create a more broadly felt stake in peace and
deny nourishment to the violent extremists who feed on
deprivation. Increased commerce and investment will diminish
the mistrust that has long divided governments and prevent
sectors from working together for their mutual benefit and that
of their societies."*

Madeleine Albright

Following the scourge of Israeli-Palestinian violence
which began on September 29, 2000 and the horrific loss of life
during Intifada II, the often heard phrase "Oslo is dead, long
live..." had captured the attention of the media. Certainly, the
Oslo Agreement of 1993, was severely wounded with deafening
accusations of dishonesty, naivete, and betrayal during Intifada II.
However, the proper response was not to call for the Oslo
Agreements ultimate demise and burial, but more precisely, to
absorb lessons learned, and when timely, with changes, to
reinvent the Oslo Agreement.

Exasperation among world leaders was already being felt because of the Israeli-Palestinian conflict when the September 11, 2001 terrorist attack occurred in the United States. Then the aftermath of that attack, including fears resulting from anthrax poisoning added to the complexity and trauma. The Middle East conflict then took on new dimensions as U.S. resolve to eliminate terrorism spread into other geographic centers of both Arab/Muslim and non-Arab/Muslim nations.

Ten years ago, an enterprise of integration was conceived as possible for a Middle East/North Africa population of approximately 300 million. (Fromkin). Today, with Central Asia, Afghanistan, Pakistan and possibly Turkey added into the equation, the population would reach more than one-half a billion. (p.16). Vitalization, rehabilitation of infrastructure and advanced levels of health, education and housing will be needed. The question is how best to achieve these goals. Can an institutional framework be defined and created, with a proper form of governance, to discharge such weighty responsibilities?

Enactment of a recovery program and its implementation will go a long way towards upgrading and revitalizing the spirit of past accords, and will bring a better quality of life throughout the Middle East/North Africa and Central Asia (MENACA). A carefully monitored economic recovery program promises to increase the level of employment, provide for new infrastructures, and in general, to pave the future for cross-border trade and regional economic integration.

Likewise, the sweep of activity and evidence of its success will encourage nations of MENACA who do not participate from the very beginning to reassess their position, and sooner, rather than later, ascend into this great experiment of cooperation towards stability.

Many, have in the past recommended institutional building and forms of governance to pave the way towards a sharing of ideas, opportunities, dreams and realities, all without the significant financial assistance as enhanced by MERP. A new twist of funding is called for today. Inevitable progress will be pushed ahead because the recovery act demands it as a condition for aid. MENACA countries will gradually strive for economic integration as has been witnessed by the impressive progress of the European Union over the past four decades.

With or without the encouragement from donated funds, assuredly, the validity of cooperation exists. Integration opposes economic and trade separation of contiguous nations and freezes out the belief that protectionism is a way to curb conflict. Integration bears no sympathy for prolonging disengagement at the cost of misery and poverty. Integration concludes that being part of a geographic region necessitates the merits of free trade agreements that naturally flow from bilateral and multilateral accords, and it opens up windows for win-win residuals.

Globalization, assuredly not a perfect solution, has overwhelmingly provided key indicators for a better quality of life. (International Monetary Fund, 1997). Crossing borders with trade, joint-projects, financial sharing, etc., is a natural evolution of any recovery program as witnessed by the Marshall Plan. With Europe's impressive rush towards the establishment of a European Economic Community, the common market built a proven track record of prosperity and created a stability rarely seen on that continent over the past thousand years. (Pogue, p. xii).

The same can be anticipated for the Middle East, North Africa and Central Asia nations, encouraged by a recovery plan, which will serve as the jumpstart to a rebuilt economy.

The world is on a course to globalize future cross-border trade by forging institutions to encourage regional economic integration. Barriers separating countries, long the means for controlling the interchange between peoples of different nationalities, are rapidly being dismantled. No portion of the globe, it seems, appears to be without some form of this experimentation, which has already been put in place by many governments, or is being considered.

Bilateral trade even succeeds during periods of intense conflict. The 2000-2002 Middle East violence did not impact the successful bilateral trade with Israel and her two existing peace treaty partners-Egypt and Jordan. Israeli exports of goods to Egypt rose 10 percent since the beginning of 2000, totaling $55.3 million, compared with $50.2 million in the corresponding period of 1999. Imports of Egyptian goods rose 4.3 percent totaling $19.6 million, compared with $18.8 million over the same period. (Wahby)

The potential of regional cooperation is enormous. (Bar-El). For example, Israeli exports to Jordan doubled since the start of the year 2000, totaling $36.4 percent, compared with $18.5 million in the same period of 1999. At the same time, imports from Jordanians rose 79 percent to $30.5 million, up from $18.8 million.

Cross-border trade between Israel and Jordan rose over 20 percent in 2001, despite the political upheaval in the region. According to the Israel-Jordan Chamber of Commerce, in the first eleven months of 2001, imports and exports totaled $87 million, compared with $70 million in the same period of 2000, with the year's total close to $100 million for the first time. Israel imported $39 million in goods (mostly finished textiles) from Jordan and exported $48 million (mostly industrial inputs) to Jordan. (Samir)

The increase of trade was due to manufacturing; especially textiles, and the expansion of Jordanian factories in Qualifying Industrial Zones (QIZ). (Gresser, p.6) Under the QIZ agreements, factories are committed to buying Israeli inputs totaling 8 percent of the products' value, and they receive duty-free treatment for exports to the U.S. in return.

King Abdullah of the Hashemite Kingdom of Jordan came to Washington, D.C. and signed a free trade agreement with the United States only days after the September 11th terrorist attacks. It was the first such treaty that the U.S. has signed with an Arab nation, (and also the first American trade accord to include labor and environmental protections within the main text.)

Possessing few geographic advantages, Jordan, a sandy, near- landlocked nation with few natural resources and a small, though well-educated population, has shown nations of the region how to succeed. First, under King Hussein, and later with the present King, numerous challenges were met and policies were altered.

Jordan has reformed its trade and economic regime by lowering tariffs and other goods trade barriers. The King approved the opening of many service industries to international investment and encouraged regional relationships via partial free trade accords with Syria and Lebanon. An innovative Qualifying Industrial Zones (QIZ) program (which has created 25,000 jobs for its citizens, accounting for nearly half of all new jobs in Jordan) allows the U.S. to offer duty-free treatment to the products of 35 Jordanian-Israeli factories in seven industrial parks. The U.S. free trade agreement and Jordan's entry into the World Trade Organization has also pushed Jordan into membership in the global village of trade. (Gresser, p.6)

Jordan's foreign investment has grown twenty fold in the past five years, from the average of $14 million each year between 1985 and 1995, to over $300 million a year since 1997. Her exports directed to the U.S. rose from $16 million in 1998 to $72 million in 2000. (Egypt-with a population 12 times Jordan runs the risk of being bypassed by Jordan, who has already exceeded Syria, Tunisia, and Lebanon in exports to the U.S.)

In addition, Egypt and the European Union recently initialed a trade partnership agreement that will pave the way for an interactive bilateral relationship. Under the terms of the accord, that was signed in 2001, tariffs on EU exports are to be gradually reduced over a 15-year transitional period. This signing will be additional evidence of integration and will be another component in the evolution of the triangle of the Jordanian-Israeli-Palestinian Trade Agreement. (Wahby)

Total bilateral trade between Israel and its two existing peace partners, Egypt and Jordan, reached $158 million in the year 2000, a 36 percent jump over 1999's total of $116 million. Thus, in spite of the violence between Israel and the Palestinians, cross-border trade can still succeed. Imagine the possibilities if there was stability throughout the region!

Ever since the assassination of Prime Minister Rabin in 1995 and the election of Prime Minister Netanyahu "economics and trade with Israel" has been a whipping boy.

A counter argument to regional cooperation was heard from the Palestinian Media Center (January 22, 2001) with claims that President Clinton's failed strategy for securing peace in the region was only a "mirage designed to trick their governments into prematurely establishing economic ties that would help Israel break out of its regional isolation. This has had the added repercussion of promoting not only anti-Israel sentiment of countries that have established economic ties with Israel, but has also promoted anti-American sentiment in all countries of the region, as demonstrated by the grass-roots popular boycott of American products in many states....."

At the MENA Economic Conference in 1996, Egypt's President Mubarak emphasized that regional cooperation does not revolve around Israel; that there is plenty of room for consolidating inter-Arab ties and Arab relations with other countries. (Rosenberg, 1997, p. 55).

For the Middle East, the question above all others is: Does peace bring stability and prosperity, or is it prosperity that encourages peace and stability? The answer - it can go either way, and avenues must be sought to let all approaches surface. However, it has become clear that the peace process cannot and should not primarily be driven by economics. Rather economics can best be employed as the dynamic crutch to sustain self-sufficiency, and thus self-pride. Economic comprehension is most effective in reaching its goals when placed in a proper political context. Similarly, when pushing a political settlement, it is necessary to know the economic direction that one wishes to pursue. (Shimon Peres' NEW MIDDLE EAST concept following the Oslo 1993 Accord signing on the White House lawn was based on cross-border trade as the glue for peace (Peres). Today, most experts believe that his approach was over ambitious, naïve, and impractical).

ECONOMIC REFORM IN THE MIDDLE EAST COMMUNITY

While structural and macroeconomic reforms have helped streamline several Middle East Community nations, the region is still searching for the benefits of sustained growth and productivity. Although a number of countries have embarked on economic reforms over the past years, the growth rate of these economies has been disappointing, barely keeping pace with population growth. What this means in actual terms is that on a per capita basis, people have not seen their incomes grow, indeed in some cases, incomes have even declined.

The Arab Human Development Report 2002, produced by the United Nations, was prepared by Arab intellectuals. It warned that Arab societies are being crippled by a lack of political freedom and an isolation from the world of ideas that stifles creativity. (UNDP)

Countries throughout the Middle East region have failed to adjust to the decline in oil revenues and associated financial remittances. Even with reform efforts, there has been little growth and investment opportunities. The public sector continues to consume as much as 40-50 percent of government gross domestic output and employment. This is further exacerbated by continuing expenditures on military and social services. Consequently, the predominance of state-controlled sectors pulls down the economies in the region.

Furthermore, the slow growth has resulted in the inadequacies of the private sector, which shies away from global integration and is underdeveloped. Private sector investment as a share of total investment in the economy is 40-45 percent lower than other parts of Africa and particularly low when compared to the 75-80 percent in Latin America and East Asia. It is time for the gradual and selective integration of the Middle East/North Africa and Central Asia nations into the world economy. "While oil income has transformed the landscapes of some Arab countries, the region remains richer than it is developed. Per capita income growth has shrunk in the last 20 years to a level just above that of sub-Saharan Africa. Productivity is declining." (Crossette)

FREE TRADE IDEOLOGY

Does free trade mean, for example, that firms from Israel have a right to sell anything in Jordan that conforms to Jordanian rules, or does it mean that Israeli firms can sell in Jordan whatever they choose to sell in Israel? No, free trade allows governments to block imports on grounds of public policy; and on the other hand, it says such bans must not amount to arbitrary discrimination or disguised restrictions on trade.

Free trade suggests (Rosenberg, 1997, p. 135-136) that skilled workers win, while unskilled workers may lose, since skilled workers are rewarded for their productivity. The disparities in skill among the peoples of a community are great, and many may be disadvantaged until they learn to be more productive.

Average income is said to rise under free trade since unemployment can be expected to decline. People terminated in any industry should easily find employment in new or expanding industries, so personal income and the macro-level will sustain upward momentum, according to the theory. However, there is no absolute certainty that average incomes throughout the Middle East/North Africa and Central Asia will increase by shifting to free trade.

Likewise, the theory of free trade assumes that people are paid salaries based on the demand for their services, not upon the industry in which they are employed. Jumping, during this transition period, from one industry to another will not guarantee equality of wages. The same task, if done in two different industries, will pay two different salaries, and if done in two different countries, will pay two different salaries.

The costs of making structural changes to move from one industry to another are thought to be zero. In reality, the recent experience with, for example, Central Europe, suggests that these costs are usually great. Old facilities must be torn down and new ones built, infrastructures have to be constructed and other costly projects begun.

Consequently, free-trade accords with countries of dissimilar living standards, differing wage scales, and varying cultures, as in MENACA, do not readily adapt in a short time period. The Community will initially be hard pressed to service the needs of the weaker nations as free-trade agreements proliferate.

If free trade areas (where partners agree to eliminate tariffs on trade among themselves) are to help world trade, they must try to be nondiscriminatory. Entry should be granted willingly, not grudgingly. Members should commit themselves to reducing their external, as well as internal barriers to trade.

There is a largely unanswerable and complex question of whether the world is better off being grouped in a series of economic trade regions, especially with the increasing demand for environmental and worker protections included in agreements. With the growth of the global economy, and more powerful transnational institutions, nationalism tends to diminish, fundamentalism tends to grow. The stresses and strains within economic unions override nationalist feelings - where so many people seem so remote that they identify with local ethnic groups, often adding friction between neighboring nations and within the boundaries of existing countries.

For many in MENACA, integration has rarely if ever been a driving force moving political and economic relations. Thus, by avoiding the promise of regional economic integration,

MENACA country separation appeared attractive, but in reality, it was an impractical alternative. It is time for a dramatic shift.

EARLY ATTEMPTS

History repeatedly demonstrates how a few creative minds can massage the crystal ball in order to correctly predict a future event. For example, even before passage of the European Recovery Program following World War II, talk of economic integration in the region was a worthy topic. (Rosenberg, 1996). If the objective of the Program was not relief, then assuredly it was designed to revive agriculture, industry, and trade so that effected nations might be self-supporting. One of the few visionaries was Under-Secretary of State for Economic Affairs (under Marshall) William L. Clayton who recommended a European economic federation nearly ten years before the European common market was created in 1958. (Pogue, p.224)

Another example of a vision before its time, the European Union's Treaty of Rome was preceded by the Treaty of the Arab Market in the mid-1950s. (A shadow of its early promises, the dream for an Arab Common Market was revived at the Arab Summit in Cairo in 1996.) (Rosenberg, 1997, pp. 55-56)

At a meeting of the Council of Europe in Strasbourg in September 1967, former Foreign Minister of Israel Abba Eban suggested that Israel and its neighbors should explore the European Community idea as a precedent for their own relationships. Little happened. (pp.105-106)

On December 23, 1973, at the Geneva peace conference, speaking on behalf of the Israeli government, Eban again called for movement in this area, "The ultimate guarantee of a peace agreement lies in the creation of common regional interests, in such degree of intensity, such entanglement of reciprocal advantage, in such mutual human accessibility as to put future wars beyond rational contingency." Little happened. (p.106)

WARTS AND ALL--THE EUROPEAN UNION MODEL

Capturing the trend in the name of free trade agreements or regional economic integration, historical models are sought to provide appropriate examples of successful economic communities. None is more powerful or emulated than the evolutionary agenda of the post second World War nations of Western Europe. The U.S.-funded European Recovery Program made it all possible by zeroing in on the creation of a harmonized, economically independent, internal market for countries that had miraculously crept out of the ashes of a horrific and destructive war.

In great part, one of the frequently unspoken elements in the creation of the European Economic Community (EEC), later the Economic Community (EC), and now the European Union (EU), was the principle of *containment* against future conflicts by neighboring nations (a lesson that has direct application in the creation of the Middle East Community of as many as 28 nations.) Following termination of war in 1945, a devastated Europe was committed to economic resurgence to forge itself as an instrument of governance, supported by a set of laws, to assure that no single nation within its web would ever be powerful enough to assert its will or muscle on another member state. (Rosenberg, 1995, p.84).

Those expecting an easy transfer of the EU model should consider the changing dynamics of those times. Post WW II Western Europe followed a pattern of rejuvenation which led to the creation of a High Authority, later the Commission of the European Union in Brussels) based on:

a. needing to secure the *containment* of Germany against future aggressions;

b. building a wall to counter the new "enemy" -- the Soviets;

c. overcoming post-war poverty and encouraging economic growth (in great part to counter the Soviets by receiving U.S. aid in the form of the European Recovery Program; and

d. establishing a laissez-faire, high-saving policy along with institutions and skills required to perpetuate economic expansion.

A cautious and deliberate study of the evolution of the European Union can provide an essential model for the development of a Jordanian-Israeli-Palestinian Trade Agreement (JIPTA), a Middle East Free Trade Agreement (MEFTA), a Middle East/North Africa Free Trade Agreement (MENAFTA), a Middle East/North Africa/Central Asia Free Trade Agreement (MENACAFTA), and finally the ultimate Middle East Community (MEC). (Rosenberg, 1999).

Shortly after the end of the Second World War, several stages of economic cooperation evolved in Western Europe, all with U.S. persuasion and the Marshall Plan. The efforts of France and Germany, out of industrial need, encouraged the creation of the European Coal and Steel Community. BENELUX countries were made more efficient and operational as Belgium, The Netherlands and Luxembourg were added to the great cross-border market experiment allowing their citizens to freely move and work in their contiguous sister nations. These governments believed that the moment had arrived to initiate a new path in reconstructing Europe. (Rosenberg, 1991, p. 15).

The story of interdependence by two neighboring, and formerly embattled nations, the German Republic and the Republic of France, is illustrative of how the sharing of economic benefits with a "win-win" result (an incentive that should be often repeated within the MEC) would be the glue for expansion of the concepts of regional economic integration. (It should be remembered that the present and ongoing success of the EU was not based on emulating the structure of the BENELUX nations, but upon the forceful determination of the leaders and governments of Germany and France).

At the outset, of the emerging European Coal and Steel Community (ECSC), the goal was to transfer control of the basic materials of war (coal, iron and steel) away from each national government to common institutions. Economic expansion, rational distribution and production, and safeguarded employment within the industry were all part of the plan. With the creation of ECSC, agreements abolished duties and quantitative restrictions on trade in coal and steel between the founding six member nations who signed the Treaty of Rome in 1957 and eliminated restrictive practices such as cartels (pp. 59-60) (a must in the formation of the MEC).

Six countries (Germany France and Italy would soon ascend) the European Economic Community with the Treaty of Rome. Another nine nations would eventually join the Community. Transformation of the European Community included the Single European Act amending the original Treaty at the end of 1992, the Maastricht Treaty further amending the founding constitution in 1994, a Single European currency commencing in January 2002, and social and political considerations being pronounced for the future history of the European Community. (Forty-five years after formation, the jigsaw remains incomplete, a reminder to the impatient when fitting the pieces in place within the Middle East/North Africa/Central Asia region.)

The European Community (EC) then changed its name to the European Union (EU), (Rosenberg, 1997, p.124) and became the working model for all grandiose regional trade, social and political accords. It is critical to note that the EU owes much of its success to the fact that the institutions and skills required for economic growth were in place even though the physical stock of capital and infrastructure were devastated by war. This gave the EU its basic success combined with Germany's sticking very much to a laissez-faire, high saving policy. Attempts to emulate this impressive record will be difficult, especially in a region such as the Middle East/North Africa/Central Asia, Pakistan, Afghanistan and possibly Turkey, with greater divergent cultures, histories, economies, and conflicts. (Recall that the continent of Europe was in a continual war setting for one thousand years.)

With all the subsequent amendments, institutions, laws and governance of the European Union, the present 15 member nations, (with another ten states expected to ascend in the year 2004) with its their markets and a population of 380 million people consuming one-quarter of the world's goods, have been reborn time and again as a viable model for other global efforts at economic integration, social and political issues aside. The EU's magnetic power has been seen in repeated attempts to glorify its creative spirit, in overcoming strong national and cultural forces, in generating economies of scale and, in hearing its name repeated as the preferred alternative for future regional economic attempts of integration, harmony, and profit.

The first miracle of the Marshall Plan was the revitalization of Western Europe; the second was the impressive evolution and success of the European Union (EU). After nearly five decades following its creation, the world has an appropriate historical laboratory for governments to study and dissect, in order to incorporate borrowed ideas and procedures into their own efforts, needs, and regional accords.

What is behind the fascination? Is it justified? And what are the pitfalls of any uncritical and hastily unstudied acceptance of this model? Some governments of the world contemplate the pros and cons of the EU model and are, perhaps naively, positively impressed with these arguments:

A. *With size comes strength.* Evidence -- the European Union, now fifteen nations with others to follow, has become a suction cup drawing both foreign direct investment and profits, especially since implementation of the Single European Act at the end of 1992. Contiguous and surrounding nations, from both the European Free Trade Association and from other central and eastern European areas are rushing in with membership applications (a preview of events in the Middle East for nations not neighbors to Israel), anticipating clout that will be derived from sheer size and global influence. Combined, these surrounding nations, if integrated with the EU nation-states will have a total population of more than one-half a billion people. (A fully expanded JIPTA/MENAFTA with Israel and its contiguous nations, Arab states in North Africa, and the Persian Gulf area, plus Iran and, based on her destiny with membership in the EU, perhaps even Turkey, would be host to a population in excess of 300 million.)

B. *The quest for unity unites others.* Evidence -- not since Napoleon's push to unite Europe has anything so ambitious been attempted, and today the EU's gross domestic product accounts for 20 percent of world output.   Statistics readily impress global nations who are seeking ways out of poverty and low efficient productivity. (Likewise, a prospering MEC would generate opportunities for international trade, set a path for increased consumer spending and raise the standard of living for all. For example, the proximity of rival ports at Eilat and Aqaba, the need for sharing the Dead Sea and the Jordan-Yarmuk water systems, the large-scale potentiality for tourism, rapid growth of electronic communications-all these point to a particular intimacy of relations that can evolve among people of JIPTA.)

C. *There will be quantum leaps in technology and research.* Evidence --the EU and member governments have released billions of dollars for megaresearch programs. With new EU directives, revised tax laws permitted greater expansion into the venture capital markets and substantial increases in foreign direct investments. Regional integration has allowed for the combining of people, talents, ambitions, and resources to assert a unique and determined leadership in science and technology, all promising to raise the living standards of its member populations.

D. *Regional integration helps build global markets.* Evidence -- for most of the EU's life, strong ties have been building around the world, all with determination and confidence. For example, shortly after Spain and Portugal joined the European Community on June 22, 1987, The European Community adopted a policy paper outlining an overall, coordinated strategy for strengthening relations throughout. Latin America adopted a policy paper outlining an overall, coordinated strategy for strengthening relations throughout Latin America. by building natural links from its history, a common language and traditional bridges and networks with nations throughout Latin America. (A prospering MEC will reach out to the world, with the power to export affordable products.)

E. *Foreign direct investments will flow.* Evidence -- The World Bank and other authority institutions decry the poor level of foreign direct investment (FDI) in MEC countries. The first requirement, to develop FDIs indicating a postive attitude in investment. This attitude is too often neglected while MEC governments concentrate on being attractive competitively by offering generous incentives to potential investors. For FDIs to increase in the region there must be: societal attractiveness, infrastructural attractiveness, factors (natural and human) attractiveness, governability attractiveness, and competitive attractiveness.

F. *Devastation turns to profit.* Evidence -- as nations seek ways to leap out of poverty and illiteracy, and to leave the so-called third world behind, the recent history of Western Europe is most attractive. After the devastation of World War II and the economic sluggishness of the early 1980s, many experts thought the EC had no future. Now, many wonder what lies ahead in the EU's push for new markets and profits. Leaders from around the world remain amazed at the marvels of European reconstruction and revitalization as they ponder their own decisions for tomorrow. (Might a parallel result occur throughout the Middle East/North Africa and Central Asia?)

G. *Regional economic agreements can counter other regional trade accords.* Evidence -- the agreement between Canada and the United States in March of 1985 to "explore all the possible ways" of reducing trade barriers is illustrative of economic forces of the day. The two governments concluded a free-trade agreement on October 4, 1987, only months after the Single European Act was proposed in the European Community. Shortly thereafter, the Mexican government sought a free trade accord with the United States (Canada would participate). The result was the North American Free Trade Agreement (NAFTA), which went into effect on January 1, 1994. This three-nation, combined force of 380 million people, with an estimated $7 trillion market makes NAFTA the world's largest regional trading bloc. (Rosenberg, 1999, pp. 21-23)

It is doubtful that this powerful trade agreement (some consider it a trade treaty) would ever have been negotiated had there not been a mighty European Union to stimulate a challenge and determination. May these accords, with their promises of reducing waste and upgrading efficiencies and profits, become an incentive to the formation of trade agreements among nations in the Middle East, North Africa, and Central Asia.

Perceived by some in the Middle East that the United States has slipped as an "honest broker" since the failure of negotiations at Camp David in December 2000, it is appropriate to turn to the European Union for leadership in integrating the southern and eastern rim of the Mediterranean. The EU can proudly demonstrate its powerful attractiveness for this purpose. "It is the dominant regional political and economic power, it has developed a culture of peaceful conflict resolution and negotiation, it maintains considerable military strength based on the collective potential of the EU member states, and it maintains strong cultural ties with the societies of the MENA region." It is important to recall that the EU was the primary player in claiming that regional economic integration could play a dominant role following the Gulf War, and before the October 30, 1991 Madrid conference.

The issues of containment, threats to security and peace, widespread poverty, and uncontrollable corruption remain central to the creation of a Middle East/North Africa/Central Asia regional community. The community's establishment would help to cope with rising forms of religious extremism, with threats of terrorism and with increased conflicts resulting from surging deprivation at a time of both limited water resources and skyrocketing increases in population.

Peace treaties are but signed pieces of paper when contrasted with the power of economic interdependence that achieves a rising living standard and a longer and healthier life. With or without MERP, this glue of interdependence brings people and nations closer together forming a binding force for accomplishment and success. The desert of gloom and deprivation might then be pushed aside.

The Barcelona Declaration envisaged a partnership between the 15 members of the EU and the 12 nations of the southern and eastern Mediterranean. The November 1995 Barcelona process of the European Union agreed in its declaration to the "acceleration of the pace of sustainable socio-economic development, improvement of the living conditions of the populations, increase in the employment levels and reduction in the development gap in the Euro-Mediterranean region, encouragement of regional cooperation and integration." (Rosenberg, 1997, pp. 126-127). "This partnership had high hopes of deepening ties among the countries of the Mediterranean but became enervated because of the second Palestinian Intifada and September 11th." (Stevenson, Jonathan).

The economic/trade breakdown of the Middle East/North Africa region during times of rapid globalization, can be seen as "one of the four major crises of the Arab world, others being the Six Day War of 1967, the Iranian revolution, and Saddam Hussein's hegemonic posture in 1990," according to Fouad Ajami in his insightful *Foreign Affairs* 1997 article "The Arab Inheritance." (Ajami).

Assuming a future dedicated to raising living standards and promoting stability within the Middle East/North Africa and Central Asia, promising goals of regionalism, to be defined in greater detail during founding MERP discussions, will be to: (Rosenberg, 1997, pp. 357-358)

a. present the concrete meaning of peace;

b. create confidence-building measures;

c. establish commitments that will reduce the likelihood of hostile activities;

d. promote regional and national economies;

e. create additional sources of income and raise the standard of living;

f. present an order of priorities for development of joint projects and for allocations of resources for their implementation; and

g. provide, with regional and social funding, sufficient funds to the poorer nations who seek integration but require greater attention. (Rosenberg, 1999)

THE ECONOMIC SUMMITS

What has been learned from the past 8 years of moving the Middle East peace process forward is that economic cooperation cannot compensate for a political settlement. The MENA Economic Summits were part of the economic vision of a New Middle East, so carefully articulated by Shimon Peres, that would create an atmosphere on which a political settlement might be based. (Peres)

The assassination of Yitzhak Rabin in 1995 within days of the close of the MENA meeting in Amman was a turning point. (Rosenberg, 1997, pp. 351-352). Then, Bibi Netanyahu was elected as Israel's Prime Minister (p.295). Shimon Peres's vision of the New Middle East has since failed to generate the results it had promised.

Arguably, with passage of the Oslo Accord in 1993, the potential for regional economic integration had been reborn. It was reported that the late King of Jordan, HM Hussein II had in January 1994, approved the convening of an economic integration regional conference between Jordan and Israel to detail the future of a "Middle East Commonwealth" (p.193) (this was six months before the historic meeting on July 22, 1994 with President Clinton of the United States and President Rabin of Israel in Washington.) The concept was promising but the idea faded as a peace treaty had not been signed early enough to have the conference in Jordan (a second economic summit was rescheduled and held October 1995 in Amman, Jordan, once again reinforcing the recent King's determination to play a primary role in the evolution of a community of regional nations.) (Rosenberg, 1997, pp. 14-17)

Shortly after King Hussein's announcement in January 1994, Abba Eban)(Israel) again called for forming a community with Israel and Jordan based on the European model. The European idea had similarly begun with three small countries who agreed to open their frontiers and not to sign alliances without each other's agreement. Eban recalled "The western powers were willing to give Germany sovereignty on the condition that they join a community with community obligations which would dilute nationalism." (pp.105-106)

Reechoing phrases from the post Nazi era and attempts to permanently contain German aggression, Eban argued: "If Israel, Jordan and the new Palestine were members of a community in which none of them could do anything in terms of security without some agreement from the others, boundaries were open and, above all economic investment.... proliferates," then Palestinian interests could be realized without being a threat to Israel's security. (p.106)

Morocco's King Hassan II, then jumped into the void by accepting the challenge and responsibility to sponsor the first of four annual economic meetings. By this act, Arab/Muslim North

Africa would be included in all future interactions along with the Middle East, a strategy move that would benefit nations of the southern Mediterranean rim and, in particular, Morocco. (p. 178)

The United States, Israel, and Arab regional nations began to anticipate the coming of a new era of cross-border economic integration. It was conceivable that the Marshall Plan's call for cooperation among recipients could be massaged and appropriately altered, and then transplanted to yield economic integration that might include the 20-plus nations of North Africa and the Middle East.

When it was decided that economics could be a major factor in the success of Middle East stability, nations from around the globe found funds (illustrative of the continuing potential for MERP) to support the beginning process, one that would lead to the economic summits all on the way to a promising and decidedly controversial regional economic community. The hope would commence with a Jordan - Israel - Palestine Trade Agreement (JIPTA).

CASABLANCA - MENA I

Hosted by Morocco's late King Hassan II, the Middle East/North Africa Economic Summit was held in Casablanca from October 30 to November 1, 1994.) At the opening plenary session, His Royal Highness said: "In working together with this conference, we assume a responsibility for which we are accountable before many generations to come. Only an unshakable faith and a sound vision of the future can ensure the victory of life over despair."

Co-sponsored by the U.S. Council on Foreign Relations and the Switzerland-based World Economic Forum (as were the following three conferences), and heavily funded by the U.S. Government, nearly 1,800 political leaders, business senior-executives, and a handful of economists and other academics from 61 nations were present, including all Arab nations except Syria, Iraq, Yemen, Sudan, and Libya. Iran also did not participate.

The mere holding of the Casablanca Summit, sponsored jointly by U.S. President Bill Clinton and Soviet President Boris Yeltsin, had a similar result as the Madrid meetings. The Summit proposed multilateral economic linkages, and was a forerunner of economic cooperation. One-time adversaries sat together to discuss joint-ventures that helped to undermine the remnants of the Arab boycott against Israel. (pp.68-69)

It may not have been Jericho, but walls came tumbling down in Morocco's capital. The concluding Casablanca Declaration,   (pp.64-67)   in   part   read: "The participants....explored how best to accelerate the development of the region and overcome, as soon as possible, obstacles, including boycotts and all barriers to trade and investment." Results all pointed to a strong hint of things to come; a forging of the foundation for regional economic cooperation; a fulfilling of the objectives of a forthcoming recovery program; and a duplication of the Marshall Plan and its saving of the post World War II nations from communism, starvation and, in general, destitution and devastation.

Warren Christopher, then U.S. Secretary of State declared at the Summit, "The time has come to dismantle the boycott entirely," to which one delegate added, "We are witnessing a royal funeral of the boycott." (p.69) Crown Prince Hassan of Jordan echoed the feeling of most in the beautiful Great Hall of the Royal Palace that "the New Middle East needs new things..our vision is of a Middle East without barriers, with free movement of peoples and goods." (p.69)

An Executive Secretariat was established in Rabat, Morocco's capital, in part as a way of showing appreciation to King Hassan II of Morocco. The Executive Secretariat was to serve as coordinator and facilitator and to work with a Steering Committee comprised of government officials and the U.S. Council on Foreign Relations.

David Kimche, president of the Israel Council of Foreign Relations proclaimed that the Casablanca Summit was a critical turning point: "The seed was sown for a new era in the Middle East. It remains to be seen whether that seed will grow into a strong and healthy plant." (p.69)

A giant step was taken by holding the Casablanca Economic Summit in 1994. It defined the possibilities of a regional cooperative to harmonize relationships across borders of neighboring nations. Ever nudging governments, some more supportive at the outset than others, began a call for institutional structuring and governance that was then officially on the table.

This author made a presentation at the Casablanca Summit. At his talk, a total of 10 polite and assumed to be interested people, listened. He presented that the dream of fulfillment and stability could evolve, first with a Jordan-Israel-Palestine Trade Agreement (JIPTA), then a Middle East Free Trade Agreement (MEFTA), followed by a Middle East/North Africa Trade Agreement (MENAFTA) (For obvious reasons, Central Asia and its neighborhood was not on participants' minds at that time.) The goal was to show that citizens from differing cultures and nations could enter into business agreements and joint-ventures, some projects as profitable, others as reinforcing community needs.

The atmosphere created its own momentum. The magic of the Casablanca - MENA I Summit was less of what was accomplished and more of what it announced to the world, that the Middle East and North Africa trade accords are viable and potentially profitable for its 300 million consumers.

Long-term, a Middle East/North Africa Economic Community (MENAC) will reward the initiators of the Casablanca Summit for their insight and courage to move the wheels of peace and prosperity across borders that were once thought to be irongated and impenetrable.

AMMAN - MENA II

If the Casablanca Economic Summit was historic for its evolution, the Amman meeting one year later indicated a certain permanence as well as an advancement toward regional cooperation. (pp.14-17)

For three days, from October 29 to 31, 1995, optimism filled the air. The second Middle East/North Africa Economic Summit was held under the patronage of the late King Hussein bin Talal, ruler of the Hashemite Kingdom since May 1953. At the opening Plenary session, His Royal Highness said: "The international community is able to contribute to the rehabilitation of the economies of the region at a minimum cost. To achieve this result, there should be a clear and common outlook for the future, which we seek for the region, in partnership and through cooperation with the international community. Each one of us will have a distinctive role to play in making our subregion an active participant in the regional and world economies...May God help us to achieve that which brings benefits to our peoples, and may God bless you all." (p. 193)

The goals of this summit were to facilitate the expansion of private-sector investment in the region, to cement a public-private partnership that would ensure that end, and to enhance regional cooperation and development.

The summit inaugurated a new phase in the peace process: transition to the possible integration of the infrastructures of Israel and the Arab states (clearly a byproduct flowing from MERP.) In other words, the creation of systems of long-term interdependency and cooperation including Israel, a first giant step toward any regional integration effort.

Optimism abounded as 1,800 participants networked throughout the great hall. The Amman Declaration (pp. 14-17) called for:

A. A Bank for Economic Cooperation and Development in the Middle East and North Africa to be established in Cairo, with initial capitalization of $5 billion (it never came to pass).

B. The establishment of a Regional Tourism Board-The Middle East-Mediterranean Travel and Tourism Association-to facilitate tourism and promote the region as a unique and attractive tourist destination.

C. The establishment of a Regional Business Council to promote cooperation and trade among the sectors of the countries in the region.

D. The formal inauguration of the Economic Summit Executive Secretariat, located in Rabat, Morocco to work for the advancement of the public-private partnership, to promote contacts, to share data, and to foster private sector investment in the region.

(The Secretariat decided to become a publisher of books on the peace process, its first volume was this author's "The Peace Dividend," printed just in time for the 1996 Cairo MENA meeting. This decision both pleased and surprised the author, as at the Amman Summit, only a handful chose to sit with him - including his wife - to share in the plea for and development of regional integration).

As a complement to the regional institutions, set up by the Amman declaration, the Steering Group of the Multilateral Peace Negotiations decided to establish the REDWG Monitoring Committee Secretariat (p. 16). Located in Amman, it was to be a permanent regional economic institution and a possible forerunner of a headquarters for the Middle East/North Africa Community. All participating parties agreed that REDWG would promote and strengthen regional economic cooperation.

Israel's Prime Minister Yitzhak Rabin declared at Amman, "No one will come here because of our winning smiles....They all want to make money." (p. 14). (Six days following his participation in the Amman Economic Summit, he was assassinated. The future for peace and prosperity in the region suddenly took a shift downward.)

MENA I, held in Casablanca articulated the reasons for regional integration, but it was left for MENA II to translate them into reality. It was clear that unless and until the intentions of the parties were better coordinated and an institutional structure was created, the wheels toward integration could spin haplessly.

CAIRO - MENA III

Egypt sponsored the Cairo meeting from November 12 to 14, 1996. (pp.55-56). It was downgraded from a summit, which by definition required heads of state, to an economic conference, without any heads of government. This event included fewer Americans, Europeans, and Israelis, resulting in participation of about 1,400 representatives from 87 nations.

Egypt had almost scrapped the meeting after the May election of Israeli Prime Minister Netanyahu, whose policies were viewed to have slowed the region's peace process. One of the key messages that Egypt's President Mubarak sent in his opening comments was that regional cooperation did not revolve around Israel; that there was plenty of room for consolidating inter-Arab ties and Arab relations with other countries.

The common theme "Building for the Future, Creating an Investor-Friendly Environment" was illustrated in the opening address of President Mubarak who said that economic dividends of peace would not be forthcoming without progress in the Arab-Israeli peace negotiations. Departing from the previous summits, MENA III saw political pressure being brought to bear on Israel, rather than on the participating Arab states.

"If you lose peace, everyone will be the loser. If we put the peace process back on track, everyone will gain." Prime Minister of Egypt Ganzouri said in the closing session. (p.55).

Participants stressed in the Cairo Declaration (pp.52-55) the crucial importance of the development of the Palestinian economy. They noted with concern that the already weak Palestinian economy was suffering from restrictions, and border closures hindered the daily movement of Palestinian labor and trade.

With Egyptian pride that so much could be achieved with minimal participation from the Israelis, the government announced that during the Cairo session, business people had closed deals worth an astonishing $6.8 billion. A major statement by Warren Christopher (his last visit to the Middle East as Secretary of State) was made for the Middle East Development Bank's charter. The Bank was expected to begin operation in Cairo by the end of 1997, aiming to be a catalyst in supporting private-sector projects, promoting regional projects and dialogue, and focusing on the region's growing infrastructure needs. Plans for its creation were soon cancelled. (pp.53-54).

DOHA - MENA IV

MENA IV was held in Doha, the capital of Qatar, from November 16-18, 1997. It would be the last of the consecutive annual economic meetings. Qatar's Emir, His Royal Highness Sheikh Hamad bin Khalifa Al Thani opened the session with a strongly worded attack on Israel, criticizing the hard-line policies of Israeli Prime Minister Netanyahu which he said were threatening the region's stability, "The Middle East peace process, unfortunately, is going through a critical period and is being hindered by the intransigence of the Israeli government and its unjustified backing away from the peace agreements it signed... The Israeli government must be aware that its actions will undermine the peace process and expose the region to a danger of unpredictable dimensions." While a number of Arab states chose to boycott the conference, nearly 1000 people did participate. (p. 103)

"I am here in Doha...because America keeps its word," declared Madeleine Albright, the new U.S. Secretary of State as she addressed the opening plenary session following the Emir. (p. 10). Declaring that the peace process was in jeopardy, she told the delegates, "It would be helpful if all the leaders of the region would keep commitments they have made."

Klaus Schwab, president of the World Economic Forum who for the fourth year organized the conference, noted that even at the end of the twentieth century, the MENA region is being held hostage by politics, "I hope Doha will be a turning point..the region is being bypassed on the global investment highway."

Citing some depressing statistics he attempted to drive home the need for achieving economic and social progress in the region. Total GDP had remained almost stagnant since 1980, while the population had grown by an alarming 28 percent annually. Sixty percent of the population was under 25 years of age and 40 percent less than 14 years, he pointed out. (p.103)

The Qataris declared the event to be a great success, claiming that $12 billion worth of contracts and memorandums of understanding had been signed, compared with the final $10 billion worth at the previous years' Cairo meeting.

On the last day Shimon Peres of Israel appeared. Two receptions were held prior to his speaking at the closing session. He delivered one of his most impassioned, clear, and optimistic speeches. Many in the conference hall had tears in their eyes. The applause, from Arab, Israeli, Moslem, Jew and Christian alike, was deafening.

IN TRIBUTE

The four consecutive MENA meetings (1994-1997) provided a meaningful platform promoting economics and trade as the glue for moving the region into a phase of upward stability and promise for a higher living standard accompanied by better education, housing, and health facilities.

What these important meetings provided was a framework that was set into place by advancing the cause for regional cooperation. Future JIPTA and its offshoots will learn from the Economic Summits and Conferences. The writing of history books may hopefully support the claim that the impetus for a future economic bloc was a direct outgrowth of these four sessions. Without them, no example could be drawn to show that cross-border trade, alliances, joint-ventures, and investments could flourish.

MENA's I, II, III, IV legacies are a display of commitment during the ups and downs of the Israel-Palestinian peace negotiations. Economic meetings designed to encourage meaningful cross-border activities have proven to be a viable and major source for hope throughout the region. However, "Oslo is Dead" is now heard throughout the region, with no alternate political or economic substitute on the drawing board. Eventually, for stability to exist in the Middle East, economic interactions and regional trade must be resurrected with or without a Middle East Recovery Program. The proliferation of cross-border projects and joint-efforts has proven to be the avenue for raising living standards and maintaining peace. The Middle East should not reject this opportunity to enrich future generations who are entitled to share in the world's prosperity.

While deciding which half of the glass one admires, reality results in optimists and pessimists inevitably clashing over the dilemmas of life. From Madrid, via Oslo I and II, and then from engagement with the four annual economic conferences, the somewhat straight path towards the end of conflict in the region was outlined. But it was not that simple.

Post-Oslo economics provided Israel with the chance to flex her muscles and enter the global economy; prosperity assuredly followed. It brought foreign investors and business partners to Israel's shore. It showed others that Israel could conduct business in Israel even amid security tensions. If allowed, this story could be repeated throughout nations of the Middle East, North Africa, Central Asia, Pakistan, Afghanistan and Turkey, with Israel serving as proof that new monies will be invested if solid economic agreements are in place.

"The Death of Oslo," as repeatedly heard these days, should not conceal the fact that the 1993 agreement provided the venue and opportunity for business transactions and incoming investments, plus significant loans and gifts to the Middle East from around the world. MERP will bring opportunities to secure the future.

Jumpstarting the recovery process with aid from MERP, will serve as the motivator to move forward. Recipients of aid will, by design, allow free-trade, free-markets, and, cross-border cooperation to stamp out tightly-guarded protectionists. A recovery plan to energize and commit the senior players in MENACA to unity of nations for economic well-being is far more desirable than unity of nations for violence and terrorism.

CHAPTER VI

JIPTA, MEFTA, MENAFTA, MENACAFTA, MEC

"We fight against poverty because hope is an answer to terror."

George W. Bush

The Middle East seems to be in constant flux and turmoil, so it is not surprising that any attempt of resolution to the Israeli-Palestinian conflict has, since September 11, 2001, spread to North Africa, Afghanistan, Pakistan and Central Asia.

President George W. Bush delivered a remarkable speech in April 2002 in which he vowed to lead an international effort to rebuild Afghanistan on the model of the Marshall Plan for Europe. More than fifty years earlier, President Truman understood that there could be no more effective way to stop the spread of Communism than to help rebuild the war-ravaged states of Europe, so President Bush "realizes that militant Islam and, other destructive, radical ideologies, can be discouraged in

Afghanistan only with the building of a safe, functioning civil society." (*New York Times, The* 2002, April 19).

The analogy between Afghanistan and Europe is imperfect as Europe, before World War II was a very different society than Afghanistan. Europe possessed a modern industrial economy, complete with cultures trained and equipped for dynamic economic progress.

A plausible and closer parallel to post-1945 Europe was envisioned on June 24, 2002 when President Bush's (p. A1) words of warning included "Things Must Change in the Middle East." Here the President was stroking the principles of the original 1948 Marshall Plan when he stated: "Today the Palestinian people live in economic stagnation made worse by official corruption. A Palestinian state will require a vibrant economy where honest enterprise is encouraged by honest government. The United States, the international donor community and the World Bank stand ready to work with Palestinians on a major project of economic reform and development." Palestinian aid was on the agenda of the White House, with a vision of jobs, border-crossings for employment, and perhaps even eventually, integrated economies.

Just as the 1948 Marshall Plan acknowledged the need for closer cross-border trade and business activity, if a Middle East Recovery Program (MERP) is initiated and finds needed successes, additional steps, would include extension towards regional economic integration. Assuredly, this will be difficult. There will be numerous brakes applied, but at the same time it will be challenging as clashes of cultures, traditions, and economics will bring tensions, disaccords and denials of trust and fairness.

No attempt is made here to point fingers or attach blame for the present conditions in the Arab/Muslim or non-Arab/Muslim world. If the malaise of the Middle East is caused by its resentment over decades of suffering under Western hegemony, people must stop focusing on past injustices and work to correct the future. Some people point to globalization and the selective poverty it has brought as the primary culprit for the Middle East's economic downtrend.

The eminent Middle East expert Bernard Lewis (2001), states that the Middle Eastern "combination of low productivity and high birth rate makes for an unstable mix, and by all indications the Arab countries, in such matters as job creation, education, technology, and productivity, lag ever farther behind the West....According to United Nations statistics, Israel's per-capita GDP was three and a half times that of Lebanon and Syria, twelve times that of Jordan, and thirteen and a half times that of Egypt."

Now all can change! With the United States as the innovator and provider of the monies of MERP, even all of its good intentions, however, couldn't erase existing conditions swiftly. Were it to try, it would assuredly be accused of imposing its will on others. The Middle East/North Africa/Central Africa (MENACA) region may not be the poorest on earth, but ranks close to the poorest. Only the oil money that travels around the Arab world belies its underlying poverty. Yet, one-half billion people within its boundaries are poverty's victims.

Were MERP to be established, were it to exercise its charter, were it to encourage cross-border economics, what can be shared and what steps should be taken to avoid duplicating the excess production of already deplorable economies?   By necessity, work in each country will require:

a. identifying each nation's international trade policy,

b. encouraging work with existing key institutions,

c. mastering negotiations procedures and agreements, and

d. learning to resolve disputes.

Solutions will be found in present-day economies and in the yet-to-be-discovered potential of 28 nations in a broadly-defined Middle East Community, working together.

Following, are some key economic data regarding nations of the Middle East, North Africa, Central Asia, and Pakistan, Afghanistan and Turkey: *

Afghanistan - An extremely poor, landlocked country; highly dependent on farming and livestock-raising (sheep and goats). Gross domestic product has fallen substantially over the past 20 years because of the loss of labor and capital and the disruption of trade and transport; was by far the largest producer of opium poppies in 1999; narcotics trafficking is a major source of revenue.

Algeria - The hydrocarbon sector is the backbone of the economy, accounting for roughly 52 percent of budget revenues, 25 percent of GDP, and over 95 percent of export earnings; has the fifth-largest reserves of natural gas in the world and is the second largest gas exporter; ranks fourteenth for oil reserves.

Bahrain - Petroleum production and processing account for about 60 percent of export receipts, 60 percent of government revenues, and 30 percent of GDP. With highly developed communication and transport facilities, is home to numerous multinational firms doing business in the Gulf.

Egypt - A series of International Monetary Fund arrangements helped Egypt improve its macroeconomic performance during the 1990s. Through sound fiscal and monetary policies, Cairo tamed inflation, slashed budget deficits, and built up foreign reserves. Monetary pressures have eased, with the continued oil price recovery starting in mid-1999 and with a moderate rebound in tourism. Increased gas exports are a major plus factor in future growth.

Gaza Strip - Economic conditions since the Cairo Agreement of May 1994 have deteriorated. Real per capital GDP for the West Bank and Gaza Strip (WBGS) declined 36 percent between 1992 and 1996 owing to the combined effect of falling aggregate incomes and a robust population growth. During 1998-1999 the opening of a safe passage between the WBGS fueled a moderate economic recovery, which nearly totally collapsed during 2000-

2002 Intifada uprisings. With the aid of other nations, the WBGS is barely able to pay its internal bills and provide minimum support to its people.

Iran - Her economy is a mixture of central planning, state ownership of oil and other large enterprises, village agriculture, and small-scale private trading and service ventures. The 1999 zoom in oil prices afforded Iran fiscal breathing room but did not solve her structural economic problems.

Iraq - Her economy is dominated by the oil sector, which has traditionally provided about 95 percent of foreign exchange earnings. The Gulf War of 1991 drastically reduced economic activity. Today, per capita output and living standards are still well below the pre-war level. About 60 percent of the population are totally dependent on the central government for their basic needs. Iraq is the least Islamist of Arab societies.

Israel - Has a technologically advanced market economy with substantial government participation. Despite limited natural resources, Israel has intensively developed its agricultural and industrial sectors over the past 20 years. Per capita income has reached European levels; has bilateral free trade agreement with U.S. Following September, 2000 and the violence that followed, her economy has significantly slowed, especially in tourism and investment-related industries.

Jordan - Has inadequate supplies of water and other natural resources such as oil. Following the Gulf War, growth slowed down but rebounded in 1992. Entered World Trade Organization in January 2000, but debt, poverty, and unemployment remain fundamental ongoing economic problems; in September 2001, signed bilateral trade agreement with United States.

Kazakhstan - Possesses enormous untapped fossil fuel reserves as well as plentiful supplies of other minerals and metals; also has considerable agricultural potential accommodating both livestock and grain production. Pulled out of economic recession in 1999 with expectations of large oil exports following the building of a new pipeline from its western oil field to the Black Sea. In 1998, became the first Central Asian nation to join the World Trade Organization (Rashad, p.69).

Kuwait - Small, open economy with proven crude oil reserves of about 94 billion barrels - about 10 percent of world reserves. Petroleum accounts for nearly half of GDP, 90 percent of export revenues, and 75 percent of government income; lacks water and has practically no arable land; 75 percent of water is distilled; developing huge new oil fields and expects to more than double its output by 2010.

Kyrgyzstan - Small, poor, mountainous country with a predominantly agricultural economy. Cotton, wool, and meat are the main agricultural products and exports, along with gold, mercury, uranium, and electricity. Had moderate growth in 1999-2000 of 3.4 percent.

Lebanon - 1975-1991 civil war seriously damaged her economic infrastructure, cut national output by half, ended her position as Middle East's banking and entrepot hub. The gap between rich and poor widened in the 1990s. There is potential for improvement with reform and the withdrawal of Israel from her southern borders.

Libya - Economy depends upon revenues from the oil sector, which contributes practically all export earnings and about one-quarter of GDP; imports about 75 percent of its food requirements. Since 1999, Libya increased its attractiveness to foreign investors.

Morocco - Difficulty restraining government spending, reducing constraints on private activity and foreign trade, and growing economy. Until 1999 a drought depressed the area, but more rainfall has led to future growth predictions of 6 percent.

Oman - Economic performance improved significantly in 1999 due to mid-year upturn in oil prices. Government is moving ahead with privatization of its utilities, with development of a body of commercial law to facilitate foreign investment, and with increasing budgetary outlays.

Pakistan - Poor, heavily populated nation, suffering from lack of foreign investment; faces $32 billion in external debt; costly confrontations with neighboring India and costly internal political disputes. With October 2001 participation in coalition in Afghanistan, Pakistan anticipates significant funding aid.

Qatar - Oil accounts for more than 30 percent of GDP, roughly 80 percent of export earnings, and 66 percent of government revenues. Proven oil reserves of 3.7 billion barrels should ensure continued output at current levels for 23 years. Reserves of natural gas exceed 7 trillion cubic meters, more than 5 percent of the world tota; has trade surplus of more than $4 billion.

Saudi Arabia - Has the largest reserves of petroleum in the world (26 percent of the proven total); ranks as the largest exporter of petroleum. Petroleum sector accounts for roughly 75 percent of budget revenues, 40 percent of GDP, and 90 percent of export earnings. Government is pursuing private sector growth. Shortages of water and rapid population growth constrains government efforts to increase self-sufficiency in agricultural products.

Sudan - Private sector's two main areas of activity are agriculture, employing 80 percent of work force, and trading. Sudan has significant, though largely undeveloped oil reserves, producing approximately 150,000 barrels per day.

Syria - Oil production is leveling off, and efforts of the non-oil sector to penetrate international markets have fallen short. Syria has an inadequate infrastructure, outmoded technological base, and weak education system. Her water shortage is exacerbated by rapid population growth, industrial expansion, and increased water pollution.

Tajikistan - Has the lowest per capita GDP among 15 former Soviet republics, with four-fifths of its population living in absolute poverty. Cotton is the most important crop. Mineral resources, varied but limited in amount, include silver, gold, uranium, and tungsten. Economy weakened by a decade of civil conflict and by loss of subsidies from Moscow. In 2002, the U.S. granted Tajikistan $160 million in aid (Rashad, p.xv).

Tunisia - Has a diverse economy, with important agricultural, mining, energy, tourism, and manufacturing sectors. Broader privatization, further liberalization of the investment code to increase foreign investment, and continued improvements in government efficiency are among the challenges for the future.

Turkey - Has a dynamic economy with a complex mix of modern industry and commerce along with traditional village agriculture and crafts. Near- collapse of currency value and other economic problems has severely impacted the national economy in 2001. Economic reform, a tighter budget, social security reform, banking reorganization, and privatization expansion are goals of the present government.

Turkmenistan - Largely desert country with nomadic cattle-raising, intensive agriculture in irrigated oases, and huge gas and oil resources. One-half of its irrigated land is planted in cotton; possesses the world's fifth largest reserves of natural gas along with substantial oil resources; plans to ship 20 billion cubic meters of natural gas through Russia which will relieve economic shortfall, but still lacks economic reform.

United Arab Emirates (UAE) - Has an open economy with a high per capita income and a sizeable annual trade surplus; wealth based on oil and gas output (about 33 percent of GDP). Economic reforms were implemented during 1998 oil price depression. Government increased spending on job creation and infrastructure expansion and is opening up its utilities to greater private-sector involvement.

Uzbekistan - A dry, landlocked country of which 10 percent consists of intensely cultivated, irrigated river valleys. In mid-1994, introduced tighter monetary policies, expanded privatization, reduced the role of the state in the economy, and improved the environment for foreign investors. A poor business climate clouds growth into the 21st century; increasing debt burden, persistent inflation. In 2002, the U.S. granted Uzbekistan $125 million in aid (Rashad, p. xv).

West Bank - See *Gaza Strip.*

Yemen - One of the poorest countries in Arab world, however, had strong growth in mid-1990s with the onset of oil production. Aided by higher oil prices in 1999, Yemen worked to maintain tight control over spending. High population growth of 3.4 percent and internal political dissension complicate the government's task. **(CIA (2001).** *

A careful examination of the statistical disparities of the MENACA nations reveals hardships of low income, high unemployment, sluggish growth rates, and in general more importing than exporting of goods. The obvious exceptions today are found in the oil rich countries.

A. Middle East (US Dollars): *

Country (or region)	GDP (purchasing power in billions	GDP per capita	Real growth rate	Unemploy-ment rate in %	Exports	Imports
Bahrain	8.6	13,700	4.0	15	3.3b	3.5b
Gaza Strip	1.2	1,060	4.6	14.5	**682m	**2.5b
Iran	347.6	5,300	1	25	12.2b	13.8b
Iraq	59.9	2,700	13	--	12.7b	8.9b
Israel	105.4	18,300	2.1	9.1	23.5b	30.6b
Jordan	16.	3,500	2	15	1.8b	3.3b
Kuwait	44.8	22,500	1.1	1.8	13.5b	8.1b
Lebanon	16.2	4,500	1	18	866m	5.7b
Oman	19.6	8,000	4	--	7.2b	5.4b
Qatar	12.3	17,000	1.5	--	6.7b	4.2b
Saudi Arabia	191.	9,000	1.6	--	48.b	28.b
Syria	42.2	2,500	0	12-15	3.3b	3.2
UAE	41.5	17,700	2.5	--	34.b	27.5b
West Bank	3.3	2,050	4.6	14.5	**682m	**2.5b
Yemen	12.7	750	4	30	2.b	2.3b

* **CIA (2000, July)**

   ** **Same figures for both Gaza Strip and West Bank**

B. North Africa (US dollars): *

Country (or region)	GDP (purchasing power parity in billions)	GDP per capita	Real growth rate	Unemploy-ment rate in %	Exports	Imports
Algeria	147.6	4,700	3.9	30.	13.7b	9.3b
Egypt	200	3,000	5.	11.8	4.6b	15.8b
Libya	39.3	7,900	2.	30.	6.6b	7.b
Morocco	108	3,600	0	19.	7.1b	9.5b
Sudan	32.6	940	3.	30.	580m	1.4b
Tunisia	52.6	5,500	6.	16.5	5.8b	8.3b

* CIA (2000)

C. Central Asia, Pakistan, Turkey, and Afghanistan (U.S. Dollars): *

Country (or region)	GDP (purchasing power parity in billions)	GDP per capita	Real growth rate	Unemploy-ment rate in %	Exports	Imports
Afghanistan	21.	800	--	8.	80.m	150m
Kazakhstan	54.5	3,200	1.7	13.7	5.2b	4.8b
Kyrgyztstan	10.3	2,300	3.4	6.	515m	590m
Pakistan	282	2,000	3.1	7.	8.4b	9.8b
Tajikstan	6.2	1,020	2.	5.7	634m	770m
Turkey	409.4	6,200	-5.	7.3	26.b	40.b
Turkmenistan	7.7	1,800	9.	--	1.1b	1.25b
Uzbekistan	59.3	2,500	1.	5.	2.9b	3.1b

* CIA (2000, July).

Before, during, or following enactment of a Middle East Recovery Program, regional economic integration can proceed-not only because it is the only reasonable alternative to separation and guarantees trust from all parties. But rather regional economic integration is an option that embraces working together, that squashes the seeds of hate and discontent, that defines an elevated standard of living that thwarts misery and deprivation. It asserts an optimism of a future dedicated to restrained neighborliness, eradicating the trauma of misery throughout the land, and offering hope for improved conditions with cross-border cooperation-all a far better solution than cross-border indifference and violence.

Assuredly, a legislatively-approved MERP would justify acceleration of economic cooperation among Middle Eastern countries; a MERP would be the jump starter encouraging a speed of commitment towards enhanced sharing. Then again, the incentive to establish both bilateral and multilateral free trade agreements, and ultimately an economic community in the region are rewards alone, and therefore, should not require advanced financial assistance emanating from MERP. (It remains to be seen whether some of the involved governments will be willing to participate with Westerners to accomplish their rehabilitation and trade programs.)

Regional economic integration, possibly commencing with a Jordanian-Israeli-Palestinian Free Trade Agreement, may indeed be a more emotional and controversial issue than the acceptance and eventual passage of MERP. Initially, a monetary package of recovery aid, like MERP, may for many citizens be easier to digest, for it will deal with funds that promise heightened living standards, a goal that few can rationally reject. Whereas, if economic integration is instituted before MERP, economic integration might frighten a significant segment of the population from all involvement in economic reform, fearful that it might encourage terrorism and biological/ chemical warfare, increase hatred, accelerate people movement across borders, and minimize cultural differences. These fears could possibly destroy the nation-building potential of MERP. There could be a cry from some to stop further advances of integration. Once released, MERP might be seen as an avalanche of free funding to selfishly spend internally, devoid of responsibilities to interface with neighbors who probably have the same feelings. Firmly defined borders to contain rather than integrate; to separate rather than interact, might be heard throughout the lands.

However, it is important for MENACA countries to consider that were the European Recovery Program to have stalled and not urged economic integration over the past 45 years, the powerful European Union of 15 prosperous nations would probably have required many new generations to be born and to die before arrival at its present-day fortune.

Time is not on the side of MENACA. MERP can provide the wealth. Ideas can be contributed, but only cross-border interaction, and then integration is the blessing that holds promise of becoming the glue to keep stability on track. If increased prosperity is not accepted as a desirable goal, it will not sustain the region; then there is indeed little hope for a future of peace and survival. The perception of accepting gifts with strings attached, true or not, will create resistance and even total rejection.

Figure 1 describes in the simplest way the five levels for a Middle East Community, incorporating entities of the Middle East, North Africa, Central Asia, and Pakistan, Afghanistan and Turkey. Levels progressively advance, first with new nations ascending to membership, then with expansion of integration. For example, at the outset, free trade accords that dominate economic transfer and cooperation provide for the free movement of goods, capital, and services. The ultimate, and last stage to evolve, forms an economic community permitting the previous movements, but may also include the free movement of people. Achievement of the latter freedom may take several decades, perhaps even longer, perhaps never.

FIGURE 1

CREATING A MIDDLE EAST COMMUNITY (MEC)

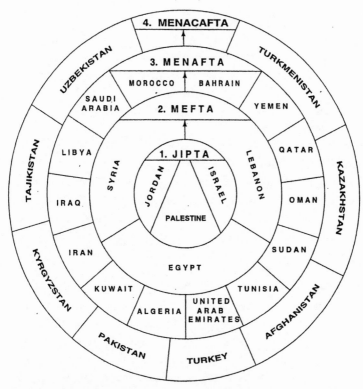

LEVEL ONE (Rosenberg, 1999, pp. 37-40).

JIPTA envisions a Jordanian-Israeli-Palestinian (Free) Trade Agreement that would function to reduce and ultimately eliminate tariffs and quotas within the "triangle."

JIPTA identifies the first step in the process of bilateral-extended to multilateral trade. Commencing a dialogue to materialize into an open trading community of capital, goods, and services between peoples and governments of these three entities can illustrate, to the region and to the world, that interdependence can be firmed by establishing tariff-free imports and exports.

The P.A. is evolving its own trade links with the common market in Europe. With time and the creation of a Palestinian state, all of these progressing economic structures, possessing rules of origin, tariff and customs alterations, can combine to serve as the model for a workable and productive JIPTA.

The previously-established (in 1995), but presently inactive, Middle East/North Africa Economic Secretariat, based in Rabat, Morocco, could be reactivated and then charged with commencing the process of institutional building and governance throughout the region (assuming Morocco becomes a member nation from the extended North African area) to encourage and facilitate others to join in a larger, free trading area, and eventually a community that someday will stretch its freedoms. (As an alternative to this Secretariat, a new organization can be established in one of the JIPTA states, recommended by this author, in Amman, Jordan. Sub-offices, responsible for discharging rules and regulations of integration, with determined government accountability, will be created in each new member nation, all reporting to headquarters).

LEVEL TWO

The ascendance of other contiguous nations to Israel, that is Lebanon, Syria, and Egypt, could form the Middle East Free Trade Agreement (MEFTA). MEFTA would be established once three or more national bodies within the Middle East region form trade accords with each other. It would encourage and administer the free movement of capital, goods, and services, but not people, the latter reserved, for the institutional creation of a community should that come to pass.

LEVEL THREE

A Middle East/North Africa Community (MENAC) would emerge from a purely economic relationship (then hopefully, but not necessarily, social and political relationships). Although an institutional structure could begin, as with the formation of a Secretariat, it is best to await a systematic trade agreement with at least three countries, such as Jordan-Israel-

Palestine. Once multiple units are involved in creating an effective model for the free movement of capital, goods, and services, a mechanism for governance and regulation would be required.

With as many as 20 nations, "size" becomes a challenge as systematic organizational life becomes now urgently needed. Forms of governance, standardization of procedures, centralized rules and regulations, etc. will become mandatory, if for no other reason than to minimize chaos and the potential for inertia resulting from confusion and contradiction. Ascension of some of the countries added to the original 3, or perhaps 6, will be justified as evidence of progress and will have already been made by the founding members.

LEVEL FOUR

Level Four, with a potential of membership set at 28 nations, a Middle East/North Africa/Central Asia Free Trade Agreement would be created (MENACAFTA). In the end, at least in theory, were all countries to join, with a combined population exceeding one-half billion people, MENACAFTA would test the forces of the free movement of capital, services, and goods. As nations beyond the Middle East region agree to participate in trade accords with Middle East Free Trade Agreement (MEFTA) countries, a required change would occur, renaming the authority or secretariat MEFTA, to recognize inclusion of a non-Middle East member. Each new member would enjoy equal rights of trade, including the free movement of capital, goods, and services, with open movement of people reserved for the creation of a final Middle East Community (MEC) and signing of its respective treaty.

It would be naïve to assume a full membership of 28. It took the European Union about thirty years to go from its founding Treaty to its current 15 nations, even though all those nations possess overlapping and often common characteristics. This overlapping will not be the case with MEC. Indeed, some and hopefully not many of the 28 nations might fail to be persuaded of the advantages of participation. Passage of time may be the necessary persuader.

LEVEL FIVE

The ultimate goal, would include the free movement of people, (realistically, many years away) and when that is satisfied, could usher in the Middle East/North Africa/Central Asia Community (MENACAC).

MENACAC might be created immediately; sufficient funding and vision could miraculously determine its existence. But a more natural sequence to unfold would demand levels of evolution: first a series of productive local trade agreements, then the possibility of a smaller, self-contained Middle East Community of six nations. Ultimately, other nations would apply and would be accepted based on defined community criteria. A massive 500 million plus population would eventually trade openly, free of tariffs with other MENACAC members and countries of the world. The free movement of capital, goods, services, and perhaps someday people, would eventually proclaim a dawning of opportunity and prolonged peace.

Nations that might be included in the quest for regional economic integration and the evolution of a Middle East/North Africa/Central Asia Community are based on four sector components:

.   Jordan, Israel, and Palestine-the entities that are directly involved in the Palestinian question and the founding parties to JIPTA;

.   Egypt, Syria, Lebanon,-the countries that have the greatest commitment to conflict with Israel that will be central to the creation of MEFTA;

.   Gulf Cooperation Council (GCC nations), and other Arab/Muslim nations, including nations of North Africa, plus Iran-the countries that are involved in the Israeli conflict in different ways, that play important roles in regional integration-nations that enter with expansion eastward to form MENAFTA;

.   Afghanistan, Pakistan, perhaps Turkey, and Central Asian countries that are interested and committed to regional integration and cooperation-nations that enter with expansion to form MENACAFTA and ultimately a final MEC.

*   *   *   *   *   *   *   *   *   *   *   *   *   *

Progress in fulfilling these expectations of regional cooperation will require:

.   CONSCIENCE: Individual conscience must be the guiding light for citizens of MEC. Personal notions of right and wrong, one's dictum on how best to fulfill dreams of freedom and aspiration, shall hold high value in determining requirements of the community. Inevitably, conflicts between the greater society and individuals will evolve. The behavior of citizens cannot be pounced upon by any regulation or directive coming from officials but will evolve constructively and productively only when openly debated and understood. The final arbiter will be individual conscience, which can counter the needs of society, but which must be protected and be permitted to express itself. Individuality must be supreme to the group. One must not harm the other, nor impose a value system that will be counterproductive and create a lack of goodwill. Today's individual, when snapped, could force guilt and rapprochement among members of the group, who tomorrow become the next oppressed individual. (Rosenberg, 1997, p. 83).

.   CONSENT: Popular consent is a critical force in sustaining interest and achievement for MEC. It is imperative that a permanent communication network be open to the citizenry, not merely to officials of the government and politicians serving its institutions. Officials who attempt to rush decisions past the eyes of its citizens may initially succeed, but the false security will eventually return to haunt them. Consent to govern is the only winning avenue to change, other than revolution, which requires coercion. (p. 83).

.   CONFIDENCE: Confidence is the prerequisite for a successful MEC, for economic growth, for upgraded social welfare programs, for political security, and for cultural sovereignty. But confidence is not an inherent right, it must be earned through clear thinking, adjustment, change, and then readjustment, with continuous cycles to follow. (p. 82).

The ultimate goal is unification (initially economic, and perhaps only economic) implying a single governmental authority and an administrative system. Existing problems can best be mastered when potential MEC nations move forward along the paths that lead them to unity. Many people take the view that without community integration, it would not be possible to secure peace, democracy, law and justice, economic prosperity and social security, and to guarantee them for the future. Unemployment, inflation, and inadequate growth have long stopped being merely national problems; nor can they be resolved at national levels. Through unification at the community, these can be overcome. There is no greater motivation for MEC unification than the desire for peace.

*   *   *   *   *   *   *   *   *   *   *   *

For JIPTA, and later other regional free trade agreements (FTAs) to become attractive, the following primary issues must be addressed:

a. A potential costly problem is the low value added economy in the Palestinian Authority (and undoubtedly also with Central Asian nations, Pakistan and Afghanistan.) Under a JIPTA, free trade would only apply to goods that have a minimum share of domestic content (such as 40 percent.) Trade preferences given to Israel, in which the share of domestic value added in goods is large, could be much more valuable than those accorded to the West Bank and Gaza if only a few such goods exist. This may not seem problematic for several traditional exports (such as agriculture and shoes) where the share of domestic value added is large. In textiles, however, some form of derogation would be needed.

b. A JIPTA has the same weakness as the current system with respect to border closures. To reduce this problem entails reducing the preferences accorded to Israel. This can be done without losing preferential access to the Israeli market by reducing the tariffs that apply to third parties. If tariffs are set to zero, free trade with Israel would not entail any costly preferences. Indeed, there would be no preferential relation anymore.

c. A JIPTA would remove tariffs on third parties, whose prices would then come under the influence of lobby groups, with potentially very high costs to consumers. One solution is to use some commitment mechanism to bind these rates. The World Trade Organization provides such mechanisms through potential trade agreements with other parties (in particular, the US, the EU, and other Arab countries) or by establishing free trade zones.

d. Moving to JIPTA would involve renegotiating the economic agreement.

The issues of who controls Jerusalem, settlements in the Palestinian Authority, and the geographical separation of the West Bank and Gaza complicate such an economic agreement.

*   *   *   *   *   *   *   *   *   *   *   *   *

Throughout the twentieth, and now into the twenty-first century, countries in the Middle East region have been involved in conflict, especially with Israel.

A policy for JITA/MEFTA/MENAFTA/MENACAFTA and ultimately MEC, means the creation of a Community which will simultaneously evolve the centerpiece into a framework of peace in the region rendering any war between participating countries impossible.

In the context of the MEC a stable economic order can be created throughout the region, and through joint Community efforts of an international economic policy, performance of the regional national economies will contribute to social justice in the nations of the region. With internal cohesion, these nations can assert their political and economic independence from the rest of the world, can win back influence in the globe and can retrieve a proper place in the brotherhood of nations.

THE MIDDLE EAST COMMUNITY TREATY

The foundation and support for the Middle East/North Africa/Central Asia Community, including Afghanistan, Pakistan, and possibly Turkey - best articulated by the acronym MEC, rests with its Treaty, negotiated by its founding members. By design, it should be general and brief, allowing the exceptional issues to be dealt with later, thereby not restricting future opportunities by minimizing flexibility or attending to a larger audience of situation and need.

In developing a final treaty, creators of this document must take into account existing national policies, work effectively with existing institutions, negotiate agreements, work to resolve evolving disputes.

The Treaty, once completed and signed, with its coveted and high status, will have primacy over any other structural or legislative detail, including trade alliances. Nevertheless, challenges, which are sure to come, will provide various pressure groups, and a Court of Justice will exercise clarity in its interpretation. Amendments will flow, as they should, but the Treaty, the Constitution of the Middle East Community, should remain as the guiding principle for continuity, determination, providing a heritage worthy of its efforts. It should strengthen the commitment to regional security; eliminate all forms of terrorist threats; encourage greater peace and conflict containment; improve health, housing, and educational opportunities; seek a rising standard of living; and promote equal opportunity for all. It needs to emphasize that wherever people live within artificially-created borders, neighbors on the other side of the boundary do indeed enrich community life, no matter what their past history.

Every significant organization has by-laws, and a constitution or treaty, either formal or informal. With such an instrument, the structure of a political system can be defined, suggesting that the relationship of the various components to each other and to the whole is explained, that common goals are declared, and that the rules for establishing binding decisions are given. All this applies to the reasons for a Treaty of The Middle East Community (MEC), with steps along the way.

The Middle East Community will become the test-run for the larger community where experimentation is more manageable. In addition, all trade accords, such as JIPTA, then probably but not necessarily in that order MEFTA, MENAFTA, MENACAFTA, focus on unique characteristics for relationships involving specific nations and identify many, if not most, of the elements for the concluding Treaty.

Creating a larger entity by linking up multiple countries affords freedom of movement beyond national borders. This means, in particular, freedom of movement for workers to purchase and/or sell available needed services, goods, and capital.

These fundamental freedoms under a founding MEC Treaty will guarantee entrepreneurs freedom of decision-making, workers freedom to choose their place of work (but with no guarantee of a job offer), and consumers the freedom of choice between the greatest possible variety of products. Freedom of competition will allow entrepreneurs to offer their goods and services to an incomparably wider circulation of potential consumers. People can seek work and change their place of employment according to their own ideas and interests throughout the entire territory of the Community. Consumers would be able to choose the cheapest and best products from the far-greater wealth of goods that result from increased competition.

NOT A SOCIAL CONTRACT

In the historical usage of the phrase, a social contract would be controversial in MEC. Under the traditional, totalitarian principles of the social contract, the individual is obligated to alienate him - or herself, with all rights and freedoms surrendered to the greater society. (Rosenberg, 1996, pp. 69-71).

MEC must constantly be on the alert that no social contract will ever find a supportive ear. The social contract philosophy, or treaty, would be counterproductive and would violate the primary and critical needs of all citizens, including determined individualists and surrendering simpletons seeking crutches. What may be considered good for society may not be good for the individual. Thus, each person has a responsibility to argue and defend that which he or she considers sound and productive in fulfilling one's interests and needs, as long as they do not impinge on the rights of others, nor adversely affect the nation's well-being. No one should be forced or be brainwashed nor to be treated by any form of authoritarian government like a child, even if he or she is misdirected or misbehaving.

The creation of a regional trade agreement and also a treaty should reflect the will of its people. This subtle variable can play the greatest role in how successful nations develop as they attempt to coordinate their goals and objectives. For nations of MEC, a will is needed to take risks, both at the macro- and micro-levels; both by individuals and governments; both by regional leadership and the collective community. People long suspicious, complacent and comfortable with a state-dominated approach to day-to-day living will be hard-pressed to evolve a self-generated motivation to join the market economy. The drive, the intensity, the get-up-and-go mentality that has been the label of the capitalist but is foreign to many citizens throughout the MEC.

Attitudes, by way of education and communication, must be reexamined over and over again. Attitudes must be tested for bias, resistance, and complacency, and must be disturbed if they are to be successful in filtering valid ways of conducting business. The treaty will influence those attitudes. Without the direction of a treaty, management of MEC would only perpetuate resentment and income inequality and would ultimately, heighten tension.

Once the people of a nation make the commitment to accept a treaty, via the mechanism of a referendum, and to move in the direction of goals and aspirations of the MEC, educational programs will be needed to reach people throughout the region, preparing them for the tradeoffs that will follow, many of which will be difficult. Only then can the giant step begin in the parading towards a preferred way of life with its higher living standard for all.

A fundamental value of the MEC Treaty must include economic security and peace security. In the past, a period characterized by movement and change, and by the totally unknown, security was a basic need that the region endeavored to satisfy. Every action suggested within the Treaty for MEC institutions must pay attention to the requirement to render the future predictable for community citizens and their institutions. Organizations must lend permanence to the circumstances upon which they are dependent.

The creation of a Middle East/North Africa/Central Asia Community Treaty, or broadly titled Middle East Community (MEC) requires intellectual honesty by demanding the basic motives. The agenda is clear, allowing people to rise to a standard of living and freedom of thought and body throughout the region via cooperative effort and understanding remains the supreme goal. The benefits of the Treaty should reach the greatest number, and should seek a heightened level that will be notches above what it was yesterday. This should bring citizens to a path of greater prosperity, to increased control of their destinies, and should provide the promise to seek their own potential and happiness.

Although bureaucrats would first create mini-rules as found in trade accords, and evaluate the results of their actions before jumping ahead towards a full-fledged treaty, that process might tear at the heart of the wing toward community support. It would be best to make some inappropriate, or even poor, judgments in the initial version and come back with future amendments than to prolong the debate for years.

Any agreed-upon Treaty of the Middle East Community will be binding. It shall serve all members equally and be the organizational foundation, the constitution bearing witness to all decisions, and be the basis for all interpretations. Initially, it shall possess Objectives, Activities, and be Non-discriminatory. A possible scenario on these primary subjects might be:

I - *Objectives*

The Community shall have as its task, by establishing a host of trade accords and a common market, and progressively, bringing together the economic policies of member nations to promote a harmonious development of economic activities throughout the Middle East Community, a continuous and balanced expansion, an increase in stability, an accelerated raising of the standard of living, and closer relationships among the countries belonging to it. (Rosenberg, 1999, p. 58).

II - *Activities*

To achieve the objectives of the Middle East Community, activities shall include, as provided in the Treaty:

1. The elimination of customs duties and of financial restrictions on the import and export of goods among member nations, and of all other measures having equivalent effect;
2. The establishment of a common customs tariff and of a common commercial policy towards nations outside the Middle East Community;
3. The abolition of obstacles to the freedom of movement, initially of goods, services, and capital, with a longer-term objective to include people, among the member nations;
4. The adoption of common and coordinated policies in the spheres of agriculture, transport, water, energy, health, education, monetary, tourism, research and development, standards, and so on;
5. The institution of a system ensuring that competition in the common market is not distorted;
6. The application of procedures by which the economic policies of member nations can be coordinated and disequilibria in their internal and external balance of payments remedied;

7. The development of a common set of laws of member nations
   to the extent required for the proper functioning of the
   common market;
8. The creation and funding of a permanent Middle East
   Community Social Fund in order to improve employment
   opportunities for workers and to contribute to the raising of
   their standard of living;
9. The establishment of a permanent Middle East Community
   Development Bank to facilitate the economic expansion of the
   Community by opening up fresh resources;
10. The association of overseas nations and territories in order to
    increase trade and to promote joint economic and social
    development. (p. 59).

   III - *Non - discriminatory*
   Within the scope of application of the Treaty, and
without prejudice to any special provisions contained therein, any
discrimination against people, goods, capital, and/or services on
the grounds of nationality and/or religious preference, shall be
prohibited. (p. 59).

*   *   *   *   *   *   *   *   *   *   *   *   *

   There should be no threat to the future of the nation-
states with the formation of a Middle East Community Treaty.
Countries are today more sophisticated than ever in their
formation and sense of political and social purpose. Under the
Treaty, the only initial significant shift will be the surrendering of
some sovereignty of a nation's economic independence; other
social and political concerns may follow. In the end, the nation-
state should survive and prosper.

   No organizational structure can better deal with the
governments of large societies within their boundaries than an
economic community. It has been and it shall remain the primary
objective of global trade, defense, and internationalism, to have
nations negotiate, unite and disunite, based on needs of citizens
and the politics of the controlling parties. It works and should be
perpetuated.

This Treaty creates a needed level of solidarity in the definition of freedom, for the continuing exercise of freedom by some is sometimes at the expense of others. For this reason, if the MEC Treaty is to endure, it must always recognize the solidarity of its members as a fundamental principle, and share both the advantages and the burdens equally and justly among its members.

This Treaty fulfills the needs of a broad membership of the contiguous nations touching the boundaries of Israel and beyond. These concepts can be applied to two or more nations and even expanded away from the traditionally-defined lines of geography of the Middle East, such as other Arab/Muslim and non Arab/Muslim nations in North Africa, the Persian Gulf, and Central Asia.

Obviously, the larger the membership base the greater the need and financial feasibility to create the organizational institutions of the Court, Secretariat, and so forth. In its infancy, alternative institutions will have to be established, but a long-term commitment should involve a full-fledged superstructure, that bows to the subsidiarity rights of nations to minimize the growth and power of empire-building and empire-controlling.

Indeed, the foundation and support for the Middle East Community rests with its Treaty, this one or another preferred one, negotiated and signed by its founding members. By design, it should be general and brief, allowing the exceptional issue to be dealt with later, thereby not restricting future opportunities by minimizing flexibility or attending to a larger audience of situation and need. (p. 64).

Amendments will flow, as they should, but the Treaty-the Constitution of the Middle East Community-should remain as the guiding principle for continuity, determination, and to provide a heritage worthy of its efforts.

For a detailed attempt of a Preamble to the Treaty, and a proposed Treaty of the Middle East Community, the reader is invited to examine pages 57- 65, found in J. M. Rosenberg's

"Arafat's Palestinian State and JIPTA" JAI Press, Elsevier, 1999.

STRUCTURE OF THE MIDDLE EAST COMMUNITY

If the various free-trade agreements and the MEC institution are not of a people, as well as for it, you have at best a useless community bureaucracy, and at worst a dictatorship of the technocratic elite. Governments of the Community's individual nations and the Community itself, must move closer to the people, not further away from them. (pp. 67-68).

Nations of the MEC should have respect for the separation of powers among the branches of government, and the full development of an independent judiciary. Historically, there remains significant problems in this area, especially in some Middle East Community nations where the judiciary owes too much of its power and presence to the executive branch of government. A weak legislature and judiciary only encourage intrusion into the process of democracy and harm the prospect for consolidating political and economic liberty.

The model for a MEC structure might come from the European Union (EU), one that has been studied, tried, and revised numerous times. While not all EU tests and experiences have been successful (or are applicable to the MEC); while ocean-sized differences urge caution in adapting their regulations and structure; while world changes necessitate new strategies indicating that not all is efficient, it would also be foolhardy to discard the model without sound reason, for decades of insight can save this regional bloc considerable time, money, debate, and most importantly, poor judgment.

Although the North American Free Trade Agreement (NAFTA) (effective January 1, 1994) is a simpler model, it failed (by design) to prepare for economic efforts beyond free-trade accords, as well as other equally-critical interactions of a social and political nature. Arguably, however, NAFTA is a sound template for the formation of JIPTA and other regional free trade accords. Similarly, JIPTA is a trade accord for three entities, and although the comparisons may be few, both JIPTA and NAFTA represent economies of disproportion. Imagine the enormity of the GDPs of Israel and the U.S., each sitting on a border with a third-level economy Palestine and Mexico, respectively. (Rosenberg, 1995).

NAFTA, which possesses many of the studied principles of the European Union, implanted innovative concepts never before witnessed in any trade or economic treaty. For example, the supplemental (side) agreements negotiated at the last moment to ensure Congressional passage introduced labor and environmental cooperation requirements, unique in global negotiations. (Rosenberg, 1992).

The U.S.-Jordan Free Trade Agreement signed in September 2001 is the first trade treaty to incorporate issues of environment and worker rights at the outset of negotiations, as contrasted with NAFTA, which added such issues as supplemental items. (The US-Jordan FTA may well be the model for the framework of the JIPTA/MEFTA/MENAFTA/ and MENACAFTA process. (Samir).

BEFORE STARTING

Beware of Pyramid Building

One potential flaw in evolving the MEC is the danger of uncontrollable growth of personnel (there are about 18,000 bureaucrats within the European Union), frequency of meetings, and passage of copious rules and regulations, many beyond need. Expansion for the sake of filling a vacuum and/or attempting to illustrate accountability to suppress idleness can lead to a sudden disillusionment and possible threat to the accord's purpose and long-term existence.

The number of employees must be kept to a minimum (the Rabat, Morocco-based MENA Secretariat was operational with a staff of only four) with increases in personnel to be justified and constantly held accountable to governments. Ministers, as issues become more hotly contested, will be called forward to meet and debate. The number of sessions must be pertinent and not scheduled for the purpose of show. To flaunt one's heightened status is to demonstrate inner insecurity and will be countered with insignificance, and ultimately rejection. Legislative matters will be needed and regulations, decisions, and directives will be required. They should be concise, relevant, and deflated from rancor or unprofessionalism. The language for these laws shall be kept parsimonious, thus enabling all literate people to comprehend their intention and rule.

Those responsible within the MEC should work hard to defray costs and sustain only a skeleton of manpower when possible. Appropriate frugality is far superior to waste; it is an approach that commands respect and honor. (Rosenberg, 1999, pp. 68-69).

Beware of Excessive Lobbying

Lobbying may be denied by leaders as the MEC rushes through its formation and years of advance, but it is there, dutifully seeking ways to service special-interest groups. It will become the means for people to try to get legislators to introduce or vote for measures favorable to a special interest that is represented. (Rosenberg, 1997, pp. 265-266).

Effort must be expended to guarantee that any rapid proliferation of special-interest lobbying would not lead to political paralysis. Lobbying cannot disrupt any tradition. Political persuasion can be productive for the MEC. Knowledgeable advocacy by a wide range of public and private interest groups can be a valuable tool for the MEC.

Since a primary goal of the Treaty will be to make goods and services more competitive in world markets, community officials are going to be receptive to informed opinions from outside, including corporations and trade associations. Diverse viewpoints can provide valuable insights into a proposal's merits as well as its potential impacts on the competitive positions of Community businesses.

Lobbying will be considered a natural extension of community operations. Lobbying may be well suited to the MEC's extremely fluid political environment, which probably will be characterized by a multitude of competing ideologies and interest groups, and a constantly shifting pattern of institutional alliances and rivalries. (Rosenberg, 1999, p. 69).

THE HOUSE THAT MERP HELPED BUILD

In the end, a structure of governance and institutional building should evolve. Ultimately, it would have a high authority-a Secretariat; a final decision-making body-The Council of Ministers; the primary body to create rules, regulations and law, representatives chosen from the populace and based on open and free elections-The Parliament; a body to interpret legal order-The Court of Justice; a watchdog of Community funds-The Court of Auditors; and Centers composed of functional operating units covering the activities of the Community.

CENTERS OF THE COMMUNITY

Functional operating units, or Centers, covering a full-range of activities for the Community are eventually to be spread across participating member nations. It can be assumed that a designated responsibility will be more attractive to some nations than others. Therefore, preference of assignment should be based when possible on strengths of request for housing the center in a particular country. (It should be obvious that headquartering a Center in a stated nation does not imply any favoritism towards that nation or people.)

As free-trade agreements and MEC unfolds, these Centers will take on their own life, with directors reporting to the President of the Secretariat. In addition, the evolution of these Centers will be determined by recommendations made by the Council of Ministers and the Parliament to the Secretariat. Ideally, no country will be home to more than one Center, but this may not be practical during the formative years of the Community as initially, there may be far more Centers than participating nations. At all times, each Center will have an executive committee with representation from every member nation. Suggested Centers are:

A. Agriculture - providing support and equity programs, research and development, and irrigation;

B. Banking and Financial Services - cross-border banking, provisions for loans, securities, investment strategies;

C. Telecommunications - planning and development of enhanced networks and professional training programs;

D. Research and Development - regional technology plan, regional laboratories for the advancement of science;

E. Energy and Environment - plans for environmental impact in building power stations, pipelines, and electric grids, etc;

F. Education - upgrading quality of regional education;

G. Standards - dealing with barriers toward regional usage;

H. Health and Housing - border controls on animal and plant products, hospitalization facilities, and pursuit of adequate housing;

I. Industrial Cooperation and Trade - encouraging cross-border activities, joint-projects, with reduced government involvement;

J. Water and Desertification - desalination, water-sector training, enhancing water data, waste-water treatment and desertification projects;

K. Transportation - developing regional upgrades in infrastructure of roads, ports, railways, and air transport;

L. Tourism and Culture - efforts at regional development and sharing of tourism and culture programs;

M. Social Rights - protecting the needs of workers, refugees, men and women, and children, and

N. Security - confronting nations, leaders and perpetrators with direct punishment for terrorist and biological/chemical/nuclear attacks.

For a detailed description of a possible MEC structure and form of institutional governance, its legal instruments, and its many and varied centers of operation, see J. M. Rosenberg's "Arafat's Palestinian State and JIPTA" JAI Press, Elsevier, 1999, pages 67-215.

The governance and structure of any large body must eventually come to grips with the ethnic and other differing characteristics of its population. One area where this often appears to be dramatized is in the lack of shared representation. Excluding people, for whatever political or manipulated economic reasons, because of race, religion, nationality, or other irrelevant background factors, should not be tolerated within the MEC.

Governance must be open to all interested and qualified people, not   restricted to the wealthy or elitists. Perpetuation of past errors of dominance only comes back to haunt tormentors. Due consideration must be given throughout the Community institutions to the sharing of responsibility by differing forces within the population. All voices should be heard and represented.

As matters presently exist, but more so as borders eventually open to   permit the freedom of movement of goods, services, and capital, the MEC's legal system must anticipate how ethnic and religious bias can sweep a nation, and how government accountability in the discharge of responsibility, especially as to the distribution of funding, must be carefully monitored. Educational programs will also be needed to teach people that differences represent a welcome challenge and not an automatic threat. Racial and religious tolerance must be on everyone's agenda.

Appropriately, suggestions and ideas will have to be negotiated by the founding nations of the Community. The "Why" questions must be answered, but the answer to the "How" question is the structure. "How." represents the mechanism, the means by which the success and failures of the Middle East Community will ultimately be measured.

MERP represents the vehicle for commencing sound, productive, and competently institutionalized and governed free trade accords that could lead to a prosperous, regional economic community of more than one-half a billion people.

The September 11, 2001 atrocity is now behind us. The Marshall Plan was instituted in 1948, three years following the termination of the war in Europe. It lasted for another three years. By 1958, the European Economic Community was born. A total of ten years had to pass before the vision of economic integration grabbed Western Europe.

JIPTA or MEC can commence, free of customs frontiers as with BENELUX (Belgium-the Netherlands-Luxembourg) or be extended as a free trade agreement, as with NAFTA. Assuredly, economic integration when tested will be powerful, dynamic, and assist in lifting standards for citizens of the area.

Time does not favor the Middle East region and its nations cannot afford to wait a decade to find another appropriate road-map for cooperation.

CHAPTER VII

PRESENT AT THE CREATION

"The only prize in the end that really matters is the prize of peace we must give to the children of the Middle East."

Bill Clinton

A chronology of future events in the Middle East, North Africa and Central Asia remains difficult to predict, made even more foreboding by present complex issues since the September 11, 2001 terrorist attacks in New York City and Washington, D.C. and the move on Iraq. One now is witness to extensive poverty spread across the widened landscape, intertwined with injustices, corruption and massive movements of frightened refugees in an area that time seems to have passed.

The war against terrorism and germ/chemical and nuclear warfare has revamped the Middle East regional front with new personalities, new challenges, new issues, and new battles to be fought-both militarily and economically. The next step calls for rehabilitation and reconstruction as venues to help reduce the flames of hate. However actions of participating governments play out, assuredly the United States, the United Nations, the

European Union, Russia and other forces throughout the world will, by necessity, enter into all future local, institutional and governance decisions. On the front burner must be the evolution of a broad recovery program. What most Arab specialists already knew has now been formally confirmed by "a group of distinguished Arab intellectuals" that only an "unbiased, objective analysis" could assist the "Arab peoples and policy-makers in search of a bright future." (Friedman, 2002).

The United Nations Development Program (UNDP) along with the *Arab Fund for Economic and Social Development* pinpointed the three powerful reasons the Arab world remains in trouble; (1) the lack of freedom for citizens to speak, innovate and affect political life; (2) a failure to allow proper women's rights; and (3) a lack of quality education.

With the present 22 Arab nations claiming 280 million people and growing (by the year 2020 their population is projected to be in excess of 410 million), and with regional GDP on the decline, poverty will spread. (Presently, Spain's gross domestic product is greater than that of the combined Arab countries.) (Friedman, 2002, p. 23). A massive international aid package must urgently be provided that can begin to turn this trend in a positive direction.

Although the argument that the Israeli-Palestinian conflict continues to be a cause, for which to fight and therefore an excuse for failing Arab development, there is much more causing the plight of the Arabs.

The Israeli-Palestinian Conflict Remains a Central Issue

Were nations encircling Israel prepared to sign on to an economic recovery plan, accompanied by a non-aggression pact with Israel, Congress and President Bush would be encouraged to respond with financial assistance via MERP. (We should remind ourselves that the October 30, 1991 Madrid Conference, the forerunner, to the Oslo Accords, was the product of intensive political efforts, carried out in the region immediately following the Gulf War. It was initiated by President George Bush Sr.) (Rosenberg, 1997, pp.269-270).

Unfortunately, dreams of better times for the Palestinians, encouraged by the signing of the Oslo Accord in 1993, were largely shattered after the failure of the Camp David talks at the end of the Clinton Administration in December 2000. Expectations of an economic rebirth throughout the West Bank and Gaza have evaporated. Indeed, conditions are worse today than they were in the nineties. Hope has turned to hopelessness.

Rather than continuing to harp on the protective carapace of a discredited and dormant Oslo, it is imperative that future movements and recommendations be linked to realities of the Middle East and greater region based on current events in the year 2003.

Exacerbating the situation, charred by months of violence at the end of the year 2000 and throughout 2002, all involved parties in Israel and the PA claim to seek resolution. The problem is that the perceptions of justice and compromise differ considerably, based on history, culture, religion, and trust, or more specifically, lack of trust. Inevitably, and the sooner the better, the Middle East, with all of its arrogance, must exhaust itself and turn to a closure, not of its borders, but of its latest horrific, chapter of violence and confrontation.

The post-January 2003 - second term government of Israel's Prime Minister Sharon, with considerable engagement from President George W. Bush, Secretary of State Colin Powell, the United Nations, the European Union, Russia, and the United Nations seeks to find the means for stroking the paths of opportunity, worn out by the freeze of past decades.

As this author sees it, the United States will continue to play the primary leadership role, albeit sharing it with others. The United States may no longer enjoy the prestigious seat atop the pyramid; the pinnacle of being "honest broker" has worn thin and others await the chance to emerge as the new mediators searching for the correct fix. There will also be a formula to move forward with financial assistance, all intended to protect the stability of the region, and consequently, the rest of the world.

Others may also offer some aid, but U.S. direction from Washington shall come swiftly. The window of opportunity, open for a brief timeslot, can provide the avenue towards a permanent finale to this crisis of long-standing. The United States, a third party at best, can steer the antagonists to end a sad chapter in their tumultuous history by showing that it will commit significant monies of assistance to the region.   As part of the vision for tomorrow, blessed with chances for greater prosperity and projected opportunities, a summary of the principle elements of the recovery plan include:

A. The promise of peace accords with hopes for financial assistance

The Marshall Plan was conceived as an act of humanity and strategy to sustain democracy in Western Europe. For its day, it was an expensive, ingenious program of $17 billion (only $13 billion was used) that accomplished its objectives. (McCullough, pp. 579-580).

Now, with only two Arab nations, Egypt and Jordan, having peace treaties with Israel, efforts to return to a once glorious neighborhood, with its splendid history, culture, and prosperity, are pivotal to the negotiated conclusion of violence and hostilities with governments of the Israelis and the Palestinians. With the Madrid and Oslo meetings of the early 1990s, most of the promises of initial financial aid have been fulfilled. More assuredly is coming. The world is determined to play its role, with the United States taking a leadership position, to deliver the monies to serve as the glue for both short- and long-term stability.

B. The Middle East Recovery Program process

MERP will be the world's second most generous regional aid effort (the first was the 1948 European Recovery Program - the Marshall Plan). It will be created to ensure an end to conflict and resulting misery, to provide the institutional structure and governance for its own evolution, to create success models and forms of regional economic integration, to share long-term possibilities, and to resettle and compensate refugees and those expelled from their homelands. There will be ample proof that win-win situations are on the horizon once the benefits to the greater societies are envisioned and supported.

The Marshall Plan, in its formal three-years of existence, struck the venue for rebuilding, reconstruction, and resurrection. A Middle East Recovery Program, envisioned by the few, voted upon by a greater number, carried out by a well-trained and dedicated body of even more people, will reach out to millions awaiting the chance to fulfill their dreams and destinies.

C. Participation from nations of the Middle East, North Africa, Central Asia, Pakistan, Afghanistan and Turkey

The call to the assembly of MENACA countries with their 500 million citizens will echo with optimism. At a summit of leaders, surrounded by experts and advisors, the charge of responsibility will be laid out to help those that attempt to help themselves. The models from histories past shall be reviewed, including the wise counsel of Jean Monnet, Harry S Truman, George C. Marshall, all to interact with the visionaries of the present MENACA. The hushed chambers will applaud the gallant heroes who presently demonstrate their commitment to a love of neighborhood, to a preservation of culture and religion, a demonstration of crossing borders in peace and opportunity as a hopeful direction for any region.

What may be considered naïve or untested by some critics will find a larger audience willing to explore multiple options and models so that front page headlines may one day shift from coverage of destruction to descriptions of stability and development.

D. An extensive review of national needs and national contribution

The summit gathering will deliver homework to the support staff of participating countries. They in turn, with forms, outlines, and surveys in hand, will identify existing national needs and resources within their boundaries, along with the necessary supportive data to make their convincing argument. At all times, counsel will be provided by Washington to guide these decision-makers towards uniformity. A business plan of usage and monitoring will be sought and found.

E. Compensating and repatriating Palestinian refugees, funding Israeli settlers leaving the West Bank/Gaza, compensating Israeli Jews for confiscated properties

It is estimated that some 600,000 Arabs left Israel in 1948 when war started. In stark contrast, it is also believed that more than 600,000 Jews were driven from their homes in Arab countries. (Levin, 2000). However, it is mandatory that no cross-trading should occur with one payment to a Jew subtracting for one payment for a Palestinian, or vice-versa. Each case by the complexities of action and reaction, must be evaluated on its own merit.

Certainly, any resolution of this enormous and complex issue, will require huge sums of money. To aid refugees and displaced persons, institutions must be created to move the process forward. Consequently, it can be expected that the MERP Act will include major funds for the noble efforts herein mentioned.

F. Qualifying for assistance

The mechanism can be outlined, first by studying the forms for information and compliance, as submitted to Congressional committees that were involved in the European Recovery Program. They then should be adjusted and revised to meet current needs.

Recommended forms must be circulated to all interested parties, whether they initially qualify or not. Copies should be freely offered to interested nations and agencies of any government to enable the world's bystanders to witness history in the making. Most, if not all sessions of inquiry and study will be transparent, with government accountability, as well as open to cameras and the media.

A series of reports will be prepared for both the U.S. Senate and the House of Representatives. Subcommittees charged with these responsibilities will deliver testimony when requested, will hold internal and external meetings to share progress and information, and will prepare final reports for the President.

G. A Bill prepared by the President of the United States

The President will have the responsibility for steering the Bill through Congress, all in preparation of testimony, debate, alterations, final vote, and hopefully, passage of legislation creating the Middle East Recovery Program Act.

Working with counsel, advisors and other appropriate committees and specialists, a Bill following Congressional guidelines will be compiled to enter the channels on the way to a vote in Congress.

H. Hearings before the U.S. Senate and U.S. House

Hearings will be held by appropriate committees in both the U.S. Senate and House of Representatives. Testimony will be taken, recommendations offered, and compromises made for a final version of the Bill.

I. Revision, preparation of final legislation, vote of Congress, and President's signature

Following revisions and required changes from both the Senate and House of Representatives, the final draft will be made, and at the appropriate time, presented for formal debate, vote in Congress, and Presidential signature.

J. Institutionalizing Congressional findings, along with the Administrator and key officials, in U.S. and the MENACA region

Once enacted, the Presidential candidate for Administrator should be announced. Facilities and the hiring of personnel shall go forward. Special care must be given to the choice of an Assistant Administrator and representatives in the

Middle East Community headquarters, and other appointments in nations where aid and project development is to be discharged.

K. Initial funds to be released with transparency and with accounting procedures established, all monitored

As empowered by Congress and the Act, it is essential that all released funds have an accountable audit trail, with full entry of expenditures, listed and reviewed. A timetable and calendar of events for each nation are to be presented on a continuous basis to the Administrator, who will, along with his advisory groups, decide on the merits and costs of the projects. Approval must be made by the Administrator, or by his or her representative, and transmitted immediately to the coordinator in each nation, as well as to directors in all other participating countries.

L. Study of expenditures, along with impact and results are constantly fed back to Congress and the President, the UnitedNations, and the European Union

The impact of spending is, at all times, to be considered paramount to fulfilling the intents, goals, accountability, requirements, and obligations of the MERP Act. Visiting teams are to review on-site project development and assess the fulfillment of expectations from proposals to determine whether commitments have been met. Standards of accomplishment should as best as possible, be consistently applied for all nations and projects evaluated. Results are to be fed back to the Administrator, to coordinators for each respective nation, and to appropriate United Nations officials.

M. Potential new members are to be considered and evaluated, with rapid decisions made for their eligibility and acceptance.

Ideally, all of the twenty-eight nations of the region will participate in the opening conference designed to solicit support as well as recipients of MERP funding. As argued earlier, although all applying nations may not qualify, either initially, or at all (for example, some will have too much wealth and/or some will refuse to establish a peaceful, non-aggression position with Israel), they should all be invited.

Once set in place, potentially-eligible nations should receive documentation describing the progress and success record, country by country, resulting from inclusion with MERP. Each non-member nation should be encouraged to apply and become eligible for funding. Of course, any nation may join and not receive MERP funding-this scenario would occur if their resources are sufficient to achieve national prosperity and stability without MERP assistance.

Each country in the region should be given a window of time within which to join, with a set closing date for participation. Whether it be funding from MERP or ascension into a regional economic integration enterprise, every effort should be made to publicize the acceptance for any new member.

N. As soon as possible, but no later than one year from implementation of the MERP Act, the Administrator should proceed to advance the principles of regional economic integration in the Middle East and eventually throughout the Middle East, North Africa and Central Asia.

Although not dependent on passage of the MERP Act, regional economic integration in the MENACA would be advanced by its passage. Certainly the approach presented negates any future possibility for economic separation but instead encourages unification to evolve win-win situations. Cross-border trade, investments, joint-projects etc., would be the first step to establishing increased exchanges and cooperation. It might initially evolve with free trade agreements, as identified by JIPTA-the Jordanian-Israeli-Palestinian (Free) Trade Agreement, followed by other nations ascending from the Middle East. The larger grouping, now to include membership drawn from Egypt, Lebanon, and possibly Syria, would be the foundation for a Middle East Free Trade Agreement. Once success is acclaimed by one or more participants, other countries from the Middle East, from North Africa, from Central Asia, Pakistan, Afghanistan and possibly Turkey (they need not await all Middle East nations joining) will apply for inclusion.

At this stage, MENAFTA would replace all former accords. The Middle East/North Africa Free Trade Agreement, with Arab nations, plus Israel and Iran, could create a Middle East/North Africa Community (MENAC).

Lastly, MENACAFTA-the Middle East/North Africa/Central Asia Free Trade Agreement including as many as 28 countries, would become the forerunner of MEC-the Middle East Community. At that time, this ingenious model of cooperation would prepare more than one-half billion citizens of these nations for a renewed prosperity in the region that would serve as the glue for stability and the window of future promise.

O. Financial aid can be terminated as well as amended, also possibly extended-following proper debate and legislation

As detailed in the European Recovery Program of 1948, a means should be provided to allow for the cancellation or amending of US financial assistance, to a particular nation, for a specific project, or indeed if judged so, the entire program. Hopefully, there will be no need to terminate funding to any country once they have been cleared for ascension.

However, should it be necessary to withhold funding, a mechanism must be instituted, along with conditions and procedures for reducing, or eliminating U.S. funding.

The promise of success, accompanied by increased prosperity should serve as the catalyst for fairness, honesty, and trust.

MADE IN THE MIDDLE EAST

At Casablanca Economic Summit, Stanley Fischer, the multi-skilled Deputy Managing Director of the Washington, D.C.-based International Monetary Fund asserted (Rosenberg, 1999, p. 44) that the "region has great economic potential. To exploit that potential, it is necessary both for countries, to follow the right policies and to build an institutional infrastructure to support growth and cooperation." These words of promise were spoken more than five years before Intifada II of 2000-2001; the optimism is long gone, replaced with hopelessness and despair. The euphoria, once a dream of opportunity, is downgraded with the New Middle East vanquished as unrealistic, and for some, undesirable.

Nevertheless, during the height of chance, in the mid-1990s, the Middle East Economic Strategy Group had already proclaimed "Made in the Middle East" (p. 280) as the appropriate symbol of the promise for tomorrow. Arguably, it was and remains a powerful idea whose time has arrived. With help from funds of the U.S.-sponsored Middle East Recovery Program, cooperation will come only after considerable argument, after an abundance of heated debate, and even a few failures. Eventually, MEC will institutionalize itself and move ever so gradually through its stages: initially JIPTA, followed by MEFTA, MENAFTA and MENACAFTA.

These trade agreements will not evolve easily, as mistrusts and counter accusations of imperialism, colonization, loss of sovereignty, and so on, will be heard time and again. As a proposed regional economic integration effort, the pull between protectionists and free-traders will be severe. In the end, thanks to the thrust from MERP, free traders will win out.

Institutional restructuring is difficult enough when it involves merging of organizations of differing products and values. No historic evidence, to date, has shown that it can more-readily or more-easily be done with independent nations, determined to hold on to their powers, governments, traditions, and cultural heritage.

Based on emergency need, MERP will initially direct its attention to the Palestinians. Soon after, it should where appropriate exam the conditions of the remaining triangle of Israel, including the Hashemite Kingdom of Jordan, to form a loose, cooperative association, thus creating the first full stage of free-trade accords that will be the harbinger of the extended Middle East Community. Indeed, the process started when in May 1995, Jordan and the Palestinian Authority signed their first detailed trade accord, defining terms for shipments across the Jordan River under a preferential tariff system, thereby preparing the way toward the goal of free trade between the Palestinians and Jordanians. (Rosenberg, p. 245).

A successful launching of JIPTA will more than adequately communicate to the rest of the Arab/Muslim and non-Arab/Muslim nations that the idea for a common market can be both realistic and productive. If Jordanians and Palestinians illustrate to other contiguous states that they are able to benefit from an alliance with the Israelis, as well as Jordanians with the Palestinians, and the Palestinians with Jordanians, without being swallowed or made to play a secondary role, then others will rush to participate.

It will not be easy to release the energies from differing nations. Many of the countries of MEC are still dominated by state bureaucrats who have only a cursory grasp of modern economics and market realities, and little political will to institute the changes necessary to realize the enormous benefits awaiting those willing to open up their economies and liberalize trade.

LEARNING FROM HISTORY

Pitfalls will have to be avoided whenever possible. Lest we forget, prior to the European Union's proclaimed "moment in history," January 1, 1993, (Rosenberg, 1999, p. 219) the rhetoric in its closing months provided signs of a block to international trade rather than the flow of an international trading bloc. With the passage of time and another promise for a "moment in history," the world will also learn how disenchanted many Europeans are with the single currency that exploded on the scene January 1, 2002.

As politicians were embellishing lofty visions, in the early 1990s, Europe had slipped backward into old habits of increasing state control of the economy, where what one knows frequently continues to play second fiddle to who one knows. Nations of the MENACA must avoid this trap of too much internal focus that only leads to impotence and failure.

The millenium globalization debates were highlighted in the media beginning in 1999, with the well-publicized street confrontations in Seattle, Washington, DC, Davos, Doha, Geneva, Genoa, Calgary, New York City, and elsewhere, and they will be repeated as cross-border activities emerge. As part of the present anti-globalization mood, some of the MENACA nations are alert to both environmental and worker needs, and they will energize all efforts to protect the public, while others may disregard these issues. The protests against the World Bank, the International Monetary Fund, the 2001 Switzerland meeting of the World Economic Forum, the November 2001 Qatar session of the World Trade Organization purporting to set a new round for increasing global trade, to mention but a few, are symptoms of a growing backlash against the perceived "haves" for stealing the future away from the perceived "have nots."

POLITICAL UNION

The part of a future MEC that most people will find hardest to visualize is the idea of a Community reaching out to the world with a united mind, a single will. Though differing by degree throughout the region, member nations represent separate nationalisms. Although they appear to have diminished in strength, they have not disappeared, nor will they, nor should they. People from different countries display different feelings toward their historic past, their cultures, outside influences, and their issues of domination. (pp. 219-220).

A WORD OF CAUTION

Organizationally, the MENACA Community will require a home base, established physically in one country (rotation on a pre-set basis is impractical and inefficient). The dedication of the employed bureaucrats must be centered on their loyalties to the Community and not to their individual home-nation.

Every effort should be made to minimize the tempting growth of employees who will be needed to run the Community. For example, many people will be required to translate the weighty documents that evolve during and following deliberations. Unlike the eleven official languages of the 15-member European Union, (additional languages will follow with new countries ascending from central and eastern Europe), MEC will commence with only three languages (English, Arabic, and Hebrew) and when fully extended, will remain at three. Inevitably, the Community, over the passage of time, will create and disseminate its own lexicon, but this level of bureaucracy should be kept to a minimum.

In the search of a fuller and more united MEC, "deepening" (Rosenberg, 1993, p. 86) is the process whereby member nations of the growing Community move toward greater political union. The issue becomes increasingly complex when the original members of JIPTA are both encouraged and discouraged to add newer nations (Syria, Lebanon, and Egypt) to their ranks, followed by others. (The further from the core, the wider the cultural and historical differences which can cause additional barriers.)

Nevertheless, numerous leaders from non-Community nations will urge joining MEC so as not to be excluded from the benefits of an accord, such as those of fair-play on bidding for public contracts, or those for setting industrial standards, to name but a few. Countries, already within the framework of MEC may urge keeping out potential competitor nations.

As soon as non-JIPTA / MEFTA / MENAFTA / MENA-CAFTA nations qualify, they should be accepted. To satisfy all, and not be hastily rushed to decision, the Community should create a mid-staging strategy, allowing non-member countries that have applied to participate in decision-shaping, but not decision-making. Non-Community nations at this point would retain their autonomy.

The cost of failure to implement multinational free-trade accords with a long-term goal for the Middle East common market would be high. Arguably, for the first time in decades, these regions are urging peace and are committed to sensible economic reform. Starting with the Casablanca-, followed by the Amman, Cairo, and lastly in 1997, Doha Middle East/North Africa Economic meetings, a significant and promising stage in the marriage of business with the peace process evolved. Hard work, cooperation, and optimism swelled, and then slowly fell apart.

There is so much to be learned and saved from these summits and conferences. Failure to initiate the admirable and responsible goals of the MEC meetings might disengage leaders, undermine new democracies and weaken future hopes for cooperation. It could also jeopardize efforts to restructure nations' economies along free-market, export-oriented lines. Any commitment to the Middle East/North Africa/Central Asia countries should be as profound as those that have been provided to other global nations.

Executives of the Community should be sensitive to excessive control by member nations. Leaders, secured by their hidden towers of administration, can easily remove themselves from the tempo of the masses and thus have inadequate communication. Eventually, such insensitivity will return to haunt the progress of the Community. Additionally, should a superstate mentality be perceived, an inevitable backlash will flow from the citizenry. Community authorities must disavow attempts at this inflated status, evidenced by behavior and documents of directives and regulations. They must be cautious by avoiding the construction of a system with an excessive, centralized bureaucracy.

These Community pioneers ought to incorporate "subsidiarity" (p. 269) into their deliberations. This principle suggests that anything that can be better done at a local, regional, or national level should, therefore, not be done at a Community level. Claiming that the Community should only act when strictly necessary can be debated at length. One nation of the region can claim interference while another can argue for needed Community action. Each government may have its own priorities that it would impose on the others.

VIOLENCE AND TERRORISM BEGETS A MIDDLE EAST RECOVERY PROGRAM WHICH BEGETS A QUEST FOR FREEDOM, RIGHTS, EDUCATIONAL OPPORTUNITY, STABILITY, PROSPERITY, AND COMMUNITY - THE NOBLEST OF GOALS

The Fall of 2000 started a horrific, and hopefully, last chapter of the Israeli-Palestinian violence. What is certain is that the consequences on the Palestinian and Israeli citizens were both enormous, both in terms of lost lives and lost opportunities.

Before Intifada II trade between Israel and the Palestinians was valued at $2 billion a year. Now it has dried up almost completely since the start of the uprising.

The Palestinian Authority (PA), having lost more than one-third of its gross domestic product, cannot be viable without trade and jobs within Israel. Economic separation, if implemented, would only lead to a further decrease in incomes, and higher unemployment followed by rampant poverty. Promised aid by Arab nations to the PA, even if fully distributed, would merely replace already-lost income resulting from the current disturbances.

In Israel, the termination of economic relations would result in a one-time loss of about 1 percent of its gross domestic product, or approximately $1 billion. However, as the region becomes less stable, foreign capital will slow down even further, which could drop Israel's reserves to half and lead to a significant currency devaluation.

Hatred does not augur well for the integration of economies that attempts to inspire cooperation among citizens and governments. Hatred also frightens away outside assistance, even from formerly-staunch supporters. When describing the need for walls in the Middle East, David Makovsky said in the Spring 2001, "A wall with windows is required. The geography of the region is so intimate that the two states will have to share resources such as electricity grids and water for the foreseeable future. The PA depends on Israel for a third of its GNP, and if regulated properly, economic interaction could continue." (Makovsky, 2001).

Terrorist attacks against the United States in September, 2001 will remain as a defining moment for its citizens. It will forever alter attitudes of complacency, indifference, and most importantly, assumptions of guaranteed insulation from overseas warfare. TV programs that tune into camps of the enemy will subject Americans to eye-opening encouragement to remain involved, to defend and to outline strategies that protect vulnerable borders and shores. Then, their attention will turn to helping friendly governments of MEC with rehabilitation and rebuilding, stone by stone and dollar by dollar.

Fortunately, history has provided an avenue of rescue. Emotions have and can be tamed. For example, the French-German historic relationship of neighbors killing and dying in one hundred years of war has today been replaced by the same two nations that are now wealthy, trading partners in a present community of 13 other wealthy, trading partners. This superb and powerful model of faith, promise and considerable trust must replace any call for separation, isolation, and the termination of economic sharing across borders.

MERP can provide the incentive and financial means to restore the Middle East region to a vitality, not seen in centuries. MERP will also encourage the advancement of neighboring nations to form free trade accords and extend a hand for an eventual community. With success stories and continued outreach, as many as one-half billion people out of the world's 6 billion, can take comfort in knowing that they are represented by an institution ultimately dedicated to political stability, extended freedom, rights for all, improved education, and economic prosperity.

As barriers to internal trade fall, businesspeople and entrepreneurs from all member nations will begin to take advantage of new challenges and opportunities and thereby increase the volume of activity. Because the level of cross-border business is presently so small within MENACA, the growth rates will be high. In the end, MEC will emerge as a dynamic part of the global economy.

Arguably helpful in advancing living standards and income in the region, MERP monies alone are not the solution. What is critical is for the leaders of member countries to change the way they think. It may prove harder to alter attitudes and expectations than anything else in the structures.   It will take considerable time for many member countries to prosper, especially those that don't find a "big brother" to take them by the hand. Backlashes and calls for a return to older ways of life will occur as progress down the road from a socialist to a market-free enterprise economy will be slow-moving. Leaders must devote time to building public support for their policies.

Free-trading partners that move furthest and fastest towards a heightened living standard and fuller employment will be those with national identities, a growing and large middle class and a developed economy that existed before the formation of the Community.

No aspiring nation of the region that wishes to partake of the MERP funding can avoid eventual participation in MEC, for it will be a condition of released monies. By this, a reinforcing, successful example will be set into place before others rush to embrace any model. Likewise, for those nations that have no democratic tradition to help rebuild their societies, satisfactory reintegration into MEC may take decades and possibly generations to evolve. Privatization procedures should be simple; trade arrangements with neighbors should not be dissolved too rapidly, and adequate attention must be paid to reducing external debt.

* * * * * * * * * * * * * * * * * *

In a golden age over a millennium ago, the region was the commercial and cultural crossroads of the world. Jerusalem was, biblically, the center of the globe, and Baghdad shared a major place in history.

A more peaceful, more prosperous, and more integrated Middle East, and later Middle East/North Africa and Middle East/North Africa/Central Asia plus Pakistan, Afghanistan and possibly Turkey, can once again take a position among other movers of the global economy, making this vision a reality.

Innovation is central to the Community's growth, not only for economic growth, but also for political and social development. Whether of a product, service, or a process, innovation is not a simple, uniform concept. It does not often happen in one place, or one time. Usually, innovation is a series of small refinements developed over a lengthy time-frame.

The billions of released U.S. dollars from enactment of MERP, in and of itself a supreme accomplishment, will begin the process of free-trade flow. Assuredly, free trade agreements, with all the promises of opportunity, have risk. Inflation rates may climb excessively, and a high degree of currency volatility is dangerous. Currency fears can impact policy standardization, one of the preconditions for trade integration. In addition, infrastructures as they presently are, hinder progress on most fronts. Roads, ports, terminals and means for telecommunicating are woefully inadequate and antiquated in most MEC nations. More importantly, the education, health, and social welfare needs are so great in nearly every country of the region, that people left unfulfilled can tumble the entire enterprise. And, assuredly, without confidence-building, trust, utilizing appropriate existing institutions, and negotiating openly and fairly, the endeavor will stumble and fail.

First, must come the distribution of monies from the MERP Act. Second, with time, there will be free-trade accords (bilateral at first, expanded to multilateral) in varying combinations between the three founding JIPTA partners. This step is the harbinger to a common market. Along the way, fiscal and trade barriers will fall, common standards will be set, educational priorities and avenues will be encouraged, mergers and industrial cooperation will settle in place, services of all types will be made available with equality as the golden rule, health for individuals and to the environment shall surface as a singular priority, social rights for all will be the banner command, and peace never-before seen in the region will enshrine itself as the collective force and presence before the world-at-large.

The passage of MERP can be rewarded with movement towards a community of MENACA, each country following on the footsteps of trade accords that will combine as a force to be taken seriously, as an example of what can be created. Disunity will submit to an order of heightened living standard. The quest for improving tomorrow over yesterday will soon arrive.

Thanks primarily to the generosity of the people and government of the United States, the countries of MENACA will enter a common market. The evidence of benefit will outweigh all the questions, suspicions, and criticisms. In short time, nations of the Community could be entwined into a colossus of supreme management and harmony, paving the way in this new millennium to a centrifugal force of unparalleled envy and advance, ensuring a broad New Middle East, no longer just in name, but in practice.

Fifty-five years ago, the European Recovery Program rescued Western Europe and initiated what would become the grand European Union, where 375 million people today consume approximately one-quarter of all worldly goods. A Middle East Recovery Program can do the same for more than one-half a billion people, some from Abraham's biblical descent, others from the silk route descent, if there is courage to collectively move forward, obstacles included. A Middle East Community could pave the way to a rediscovered, prosperous region that will take pride in its accomplishments, both past and present.

For the Middle East Recovery Program free trade accords and regional economic integration to have a chance at success, a significant degree of mutual trust and influence among member nations is needed. Once accomplished, the gains will be economic, political, and decisively human. Once set in place, the region will slowly surface and move away from its secure buildings and move forward to test itself in the open field. At that time the great experiment, whether it be based on this model or one significantly different, will gather speed in its rush to reality.

"Had I been present at the creation I would have given some useful hints for the better ordering of the universe."

Alphonso X, the Learned,
King of Spain, from 1252 to 1284

REFERENCES

Acheson, D., (1969). *Present at the Creation: My Years in the State Department.* New York: W.W. North & Company.

AIPAC's Near East Report, July 1, 2002, p. 52.

AIPAC's Near East Report, September 9, 2002, p. 70.

Ajami, F. (2003, January-February). *Iraq and the Arabs' Future.* Foreign Affairs. pp. 2-18.

Ajami, F. (1997, May-June). *The Arab Inheritance.* Foreign Affairs. pp. 45-62.

Anderson, J. & May, R.W. (1952). *McCarthy: The Man, the Senator, the "Ism".* Boston:
The Beacon Press.

Anti-Defamation League. (1997). *Towards Final Status: Pending Issues in Israeli-Palestinian Negotiations.* New York: Anti-Defamation League.

Anti-Defamation League (1994). *Beyond the White House Lawn: Current Perspectives on the Arab-Israeli Peace Process.* New York: Anti-Defamation League. *Arab News,* October 2, 2002

Aron, R. (1987). *The Imperial Republic: The United States and the World-1945-1973.*
Washington: University Press of America.

Astrup, C. & Dessus, S., (2001, March). *Trade Options for the Palestinian Economy: Some Orders of Magnitude.* Washington: The World Bank.

Avineri, S., (2001, December). *A Realistic U.S. Role in the Arab-Israeli Conflict.* Washington: Carnegie Endowment.

Avineri, S., (2001, November 14). *An Arab Marshall Plan.* Jerusalem Post.

Badini, Antonio, (2002) *Parlare meno, agire medlio: alcune idee italiane per avvicinare la pace, LIMES,* Rivista Italiana di Geopolitica, Rome, Pare II, Il Papa, L'Europa E Noi, Vol. 2.

Bar-El, R., & Benhayoun, G., & Menipaz, E. (2000). *Regional Cooperation in a Global Context.* Paris: L'Harmattan. *BBC,* September 12, 2002.

Behrendt, S. & Hanelt, C-P. (eds) (2000). *Bound To Cooperate - Europe and the Middle East.* Gutersloh: Bertelsmann Foundation.

Bernstein, B.J. & Matusow, A.J., (1966). *The Truman Administration: A Documentary History.* New York: Harper & Row.

Blumenthal, B. & Wilner, J. (1995). *Building on Peace: Toward Regional Security and Economic Development in the Middle East.* Washington: Washington Institute for Near East Policy.

Bright, J. (2000). *A History of Israel,* Louisville: Westminster John Knox Press.

Brown, G. (2001). *Tackling Poverty: A Global New Deal-A Marshall Plan for the Developing World.* London: U.K Treasury.

Bulmer, E.R., (2001, June). *The Impact of Future Labor Policy Options on the Palestinian Labor Market.* Washington: The World Bank.

Bush, G.W. (2002, June 24). *Speech of President George W. Bush,* The New York Times. p. A 1.

Central Intelligence Agency. (2001, July). *World Fact Book.* Washington: CIA.

Central Intelligence Agency. (2000, July). *World Fact Book.* Washington: CIA.

Chace, J. (1998). *Acheson: The Secretary of State Who Created the American World.* New York: Simon & Schuster.

Clark, J.D. & Balaj, B.S. (1994). *The West Bank and Gaza in Transition: The Role of NGOs in the Peace Process.* Washington: The World Bank.

Council on Foreign Relations. (1995). *The Casablanca Report.* New York: Council on Foreign Relations.

Cray, E. (1990). *General of the Army-George C. Marshall: Soldier and Statement.* New York: W.W. Norton & Company.

Crossette, B., (2002, July 2). *Study Warns of Stagnation in Arab Societies.* The New York Times., p. A 12.

Diwan, I., & Shaban, R.A. (1999). *Development Under Adversity: The Palestinian*
Economy in Transition. Washington: The World Bank.

Economist, The (2001, June 6). *The Palestinian Right of Return,* pp. 41-42.

Economist, The (2001, August 5). *Editorial,* p. 34.

Economist, The (2002, July 6). *Why Arab Countries Have Failed.* pp.24-26.

Economist, The (2002, November 9) pp. 49-50.

El-Agraa, A.M., (1997). *Economic Integration Worldwide.* London: Macmillan Co.

Faroun, S.K., (1997). *Palestine and the Palestinians.* Boulder: Westview Press.

Financial Times, The, December 12, 2002.

Fisher, S., & Hausman, L.J., & Karasik, A.D., & Schelling, T.C., (1994). *Securing Peace in the Middle East,* Cambridge: The MIT Press.

Fisher, S., & Rodrik, D., & Tuma, E., (1993). *The Economics of Middle East Peace.* Cambridge: The MIT Press.

Foreign Assistance Act of 1948, (1948, April 3). *Chapter 169 - Public Law 472.* Washington: 80th Congress.

Friedman, T.L., (2002, July 3). *Arabs at the Crossroads.* The New York Times.

Friedman, T.L., (1999). *The Lexus and The Olive Tree.* New York: Farrar, Strauss and Giroux.

Fromkin, D., (1989). *A Peace to End All Peace.* New York: Henry Holt and Company.

Frye, R..N. (2001). *The Heritage of Central Asia: From Antiquity to the Turkish Expansion.* Princeton: Markus Wiener Publishers.

Globes, January 26, 2003.

Globes, January 20, 2003.

Globes, September 25, 2002.

Globes, October 7, 2002.

Government of Israel. (1997). *Partnerships in Development.* Jerusalem: Government of Israel.

Government of Israel. (1996). *Programs for Regional Cooperation - 1997*. Jerusalem: Government of Israel.

Government of Israel. (1995). *Development Options for Cooperation: The Middle East/ East Mediterranean Region*. Jerusalem: Government of Israel.

Gresser, E., (2002, January). *Draining the Swamp: A Middle East Trade Policy to Win Peace*. Washington: Progressive Policy Institute, pp. 1-13.

Ha-aretz, June 22, 2002, *Editorial*.

Ha-aretz, February 23, 2002, *Editorial*.

Ha-aretz, September 17, 2002.

Ha-aretz, February 22, 2001.

*International Jerusalem Post (*2003, February 7).

International Jerusalem Post (2003, January 31). *Inflation in 2002 reached 6.5 %*.

International Jerusalem Post (2003, January 10). *Editorial*.

*International Jerusalem Post (*2002, December 20). *A Bad Past Returns*.

International Jerusalem Post (2002, May 31). *Exports to Arab Countries Plunge 39 %*.

International Jerusalem Post (2002, January 12). *Editorial*.

International Jerusalem Post (2002, July 26).

International Jerusalem Post (2001, November 15). Editorial.

International Jerusalem Post (2000, December 20). Editorial.

International Jerusalem Post (2002, August 9).

International Monetary Fund. (1997). *A Global Integration Strategy for the Mediterranean Countries: Open Trade and Market Reforms*. Washington: International Monetary Fund.

International Monetary Fund. (1996). *The West Bank and the Gaza Strip: Improving Fiscal Management*. Washington: International Monetary Fund.

International Monetary Fund. (1995). *The West Bank and The Gaza Strip: Tariff, Trade, and Customs Administration Issues*. Washington: International Monetary Fund.

Jerusalem Post, The: See *International Jerusalem Post, The*.

Jerusalem Report, The (2002, December 16*)*. *Israel to Claim Billions from Muslim States for 900,000 Jewish Refugees.*

Jerusalem Report, The (2002, December 2). *Ticker, p. 108.*

Jerusalem Report, The (2001, December 12). *Editorial.*

Jerusalem Report, The (2001, October 20). *Editorial.*

Kimche, D., (1995). *Sowing the Seeds of Economic Cooperation.* Jerusalem: Institute of the World Jewish Congress - Middle East Economic Strategy Group.

Lawrence, R.Z., (1995). *Towards Free Trade in the Middle East: The Triad and Beyond.* Cambridge: Harvard University Press.

Levin, I. (2001). *Locked Doors: The Seizure of Jewish Property in Arab Countries.* Westport: Praeger.

Levin, I. (2000). *Confiscated Wealth: The Fate of Jewish Property in Arab Lands.* Jerusalem: Institute of the World Jewish Congress.

Lewis, B. (2002). *What Went Wrong?: Western Impact and Middle Eastern Response.* New York: Oxford University Press.

Lewis, B. (2001, November 19). *The Revolt of Islam.* The New Yorker. pp. 50-63.

Lewis, B. (1997). *The Future of the Middle East.* London: Orion.

Makovsky, D. (2001, March-April). *Middle East Peace Through Partition.* Foreign Affairs. pp. 28-45.

Makovsky, D. (1996). *Making Peace with the PLO: The Rabin Government's Road to the Oslo Accord.* Boulder: Westview Press.

McCarthy, J. (1952). *The Story of General George Marshall.* Self-published.

McCullough, D., (1992). *Truman.* New York: Simon & Schuster.

Molle, W., (1997). *The Economics of European Integration.* Brookfield: Ashgate Publishers.

New York Times, The (2003, February 11). *Agency Aiding Palestinians is Strapped.* p. A10.

New York Times, The (2003, February 4). *With Rise in Foreign Aid, Plans for a New Way to Give It.* p. A 5.

New York Times, The (2003, February 1). *The Brains Behind Bush's War Policy,* p. B 9.

New York Times, The (2003, January 11). *A Worldwide Economic Stimulus Plan,* p.A 33.

New York Times, The (2002, December 13). *U.S. Delay on Proposal for Mideast Irks Allies.*

New York Times, The (2002, November 24). *The Return of America's Postwar Generosity.*

New York Times, The (2002, November 21). *Winning the Peace in Afghanistan.*

New York Times, The (2002, June 25) p. A 1.

New York Times, The (2002, April 19). Editorial. *Afghanistan's Marshall Plan.* p. A 26.

New York Times, The (2001, November 12). *Editorial.*

New York Times, The (2002, October 14), p. A 8.

New York Times, The (2002, November 12), p.A14.

Peres, S. (1993). *The New Middle East.* New York: Henry Holt.

Peters, J. (1996). *Pathways to Peace: The Multilateral Arab-Israeli Peace Talks,* London: The Royal Institute of International Affairs.

Pharaohs, (2001, January) London & Cairo. *Editorial.*

Phillips, C., (1966). *The Truman Presidency: The History of a Triumphant Succession* New York: Macmillan Co.

Pogue, F.C. (1987). *George C. Marshall: Statesman.* New York: Viking.

Rashid, Ahmed, (2002), *JIHAD: The Rise of Militant Islam in Central Asia,* New York, Penguin Books.

Reeves, T.C. (1982). *The Life and Times of Joe McCarthy.* New York: Stein and Day.

Rejewan, N. (1999). *Israel's Place in the Middle East.* Gainesville: University of Florida Press.

Robson, P., (1998). (4th Edition). *The Economics of International Integration.* London: Routledge.

Rosenberg, J.M. (1999). *Arafat's Palestinian State and JIPTA: The Best Hope for Lasting Peace in the Middle East.* Stanford: JAI Press.

Rosenberg, J.M. (1997). *Encyclopedia of the Middle East Peace Process and the Middle East/North Africa Economic Community.* Greenwich: JAI Press.

Rosenberg, J.M. (1996). *The Peace Dividend: Creating a Middle East/North Africa Community.* Rabat: Secretariat of MENA Economic Summits.

Rosenberg, J.M. (1995). *Encyclopedia of the North American Free Trade Agreement, the New American Community and Latin-American Trade.* Westport: Greenwood Press.

Rosenberg, J.M. (1994). *Dictionary of International Trade.* New York: John Wiley & Sons.

Rosenberg, J.M. (1992). *The New American Community: A Response to the European and Asian Economic Challenge.* Westport: Praeger.

Rosenberg, J.M. (1991). *The New Europe: An A to Z Compendium on the European Community.* Washington: The Bureau of National Affairs.

Rovere, R.H. (1960). *Senator Joe McCarthy.* Cleveland and New York: The World Publishing Company.

Royal Hashemite Court. (1995). *Building a Prosperous Peace: Amman '95, Middle East and North Africa Economic Summit.* Amman: International Press Office.

Rubin, B. (1999). *The Transformation of Palestinian Politics: From Revolution to State-Building.* Cambridge: Harvard University Press.

Safire, W., (2002, April 4), *Sharon on Survival,* The New York Times.

Said, E.W., (2000). *The End of the Peace Process: Oslo and After.* New York: Pantheon Books.

Samir, S., (2000, December). *Jordan-US FTA: The Ant & The Elephant.* Pharaohs. p. 43.

Savir, U., (1998). *The Process: 1,100 Days That Changed the Middle East.* New York: Random House.

Schofield, C.H. & Schofield, R.N., (1994), *The Middle East and North Africa.* London: Routledge.

Segev, S., (1998). *Crossing the Jordan.* New York: St. Martin's Press.

Sewell, D., (2001, May). *Governance and the Business Environment in the West Bank/Gaza.* Washington: The World Bank.

Sharansky, N., (2002, May 12). *A Marshall Plan for the Palestinians,* The New York Times.

Sokolsky, R., & McMillan, J., (2002, February 12). *Foreign Aid in Our Own Defense,* The New York Times.

Stevenson, Jonathan, (2003, February 1). *The Qaeda Vipers in Europe's Bosom,* The New York Times, p. A 19.

UNCTAD, (2002, July 26), *Report on UNCTAD's Assistance to the Palestinian People,* Geneva: UNCTAD.

UNCTAD, (1998). *Palestine Merchandise Trade in the 1990s.* Geneva: UNCTAD.

UNDP, (2002, July). *Arab Human Development Report, 2002.* New York: United Nations.

Wahby, E., (2001, March). *Forging a Deal: EU-Egypt Trade Agreement.* Pharaohs. p. 42.

Wall Street Journal, The (2003, March 10) *U.S. Prepares for Rebuilding Iraq.* p.A3).

Wall Street Journal, The (2002, April 13). *Editorial.*

Wall Street Journal, The (2001, November 12). *Editorial.*

Warren, C. (2001). *Chances of a Lifetime,* New York: Scribner.

Warren, C. (1998). *In the Stream of History.* Stanford: Stanford University Press, *Washington File,* (2002, July 24), *Hearing,* U.S. Department of State, House International Relations Committee.

Wilson, R., (1995). *Economic Development in ;the Middle East.* London: Routledge.

Winter, Elmer L., (July 2002), *Middle East Economic Development Plan (MEED),* unpublished.

World Bank, The (2002, March 18). *Fifteen Months-Intifada, Closures and Palestinian Economic Crisis.* Washington: The World Bank.

World Bank, The (1999, Third Quarter). *Carrying the World Bank Program into the Next Millenium - West Bank and Gaza Update.* Washington: The World Bank.

World Bank, The (1997). *Getting Connected: Private Participation in Infrastructure in the Middle East and North Africa.* Washington: The World Bank.

World Bank, The (1995). *Claiming the Future: Choosing Prosperity in the Middle East and North Africa.* Washington: The World Bank.

Zakaria, F. (2001, October 15). *Why Do They Hate Us? - the Politics of Rage,* Newsweek p. 21-24.

ABOUT THE AUTHOR

Jerry M. Rosenberg is Director of the Center for Middle East Business Studies and Professor of International Business at the Rutgers Business School, Rutgers University, Newark, New Jersey, USA. He has also been a Visiting Professor at the University of British Columbia (Canada), Middlesex Polytechnic University (England), Ben-Gurion University (Israel), John Cabot University (Italy), Ecole Superieure Commerce Marseille-Provence (France), and has lectured at the University of Pavia (Italy), the London School of Economic and Political Sciences (England), Hebrew University (Israel), Al-Akawan University (Morocco), and the University of Hawaii.

He received his B.S. degree from The City College of New York, an M.A. from Ohio State University, Certificate from the Conservatoire Nationale des Arts et Metiers (National Institute of Science, Technology and Management in Paris), and Ph.D. from New York University.

He has had 30 books published, including nine subsequent new editions. Many of these works have been translated into several languages, including Japanese, Russian, Czech/Slovak, Chinese, and Spanish.

An "expert" speaker at all four Middle East/North Africa Economic Summits (Casablanca, Amman, Cairo, and Doha), he has drawn from 20 years of experience in writing and researching on regional economic integration dealing with the European Union, NAFTA and Latin-American Trade. He has made numerous trips to North Africa, the Middle East, and Central Asia to collect pertinent data and to interview many of their leaders.

Dr. Rosenberg first presented a model for a potential community of regional nations at the Casablanca- 1994 and October 1995 Amman Middle East/North Africa Economic Summits. The Executive Secretariat of the Middle East/North

Africa Summits commissioned Rosenberg's *The Peace Dividend: Creating a Middle East/North Africa Community;* it was printed and distributed it at the Cairo Economic Conference in 1996. His *Encyclopedia of the Middle East Peace Process and the Middle East/ North Africa Economic Community* was completed in time for the Doha, Qatar, opening plenary in November 1997. Based on his volume, *Arafat's Palestinian State and JIPTA: The Best Hope for Lasting Peace in the Middle East,* he has presented his model for regional economic integration in the North Africa, the Middle East, and Central Asia to numerous government and private-sector organizations, including briefings at the U.S. State Department, and The World Bank.

Jerry M. Rosenberg lives in New York City. He has been married to Ellen Y. Rosenberg for 43 years, is the father of two married daughters, Lauren and Liz, and of sons-in-law Bob and Jon, and is grandfather to Bess, Ella, and Celia.

INDEX

Azoulay, Andre, *viii*
Badini, Antonio, 97
Bahrain, 156, 161
Bank For Economic Cooperation and Development in the Middle
    East and North Africa, 146
Barak, Ehud, *viii,* 3, 8, 24, 39, 42-43. *See* separation
Barcelona Declaration, 140
Bell, William, 28. *See* Christian Aid
BENELUX, 185
Bevin, Ernest, 61-62
bilateral trade, 117, 121, 128
Bin Laden, Osama, 4, 78. *See* September 11, 2001
Breteche, Jean, 21. *See* Paris Economic Agreement
Brown, Gordon, 85. *See* Marshall Plan
buffer zones, *See* separation
Bush, George, 188. *See* Gulf War, Madrid Conference
Bush, George W., *xi,* 4-6, 12, 36, 48, 89-90, 96, 153, 189. *See*
    terrorism
Bush Plan, 91, 154
Bush-Sharon Plan, 94. *See* Marshall Plan
Cairo Declaration, 148. *See* Middle East Development Bank
Cairo Middle East/North Africa Economic Conference, *viii,* 127-
    289, 133, 148-49. *Compare* Amman Middle East/North
    Africa Economic Summit, Casablanca Middle East/North
    Africa Economic Conference, Doha Middle East/North
    Africa Economic Conference
Camp David,139. *See* Clinton, Bill
Casablanca Declaration, 144-45
Casablanca Middle East/North Africa Economic Summit, *viii,*
    143-145, 196. *Compare* Amman Middle East/North Africa
    Economic Summit, Cairo Middle East/North Africa
    Economic Conference, Doha Middle East/North Africa
    Economic Conference
Centers (Middle East Community), 182-84. *See* Middle East
    Community Treaty .

Yemen, 160-61
Zakaria, Fareed, 4